The Wake-up Call

Hope for the 9/11 Generation

John W. Nieder
with Greg Enos

The Wake-up Call
by John W. Nieder
with Greg Enos

Printed in the United States of America

Library of Congress Control Number: 2002110756
ISBN 1-591602-23-8

Unless otherwise indicated, Bible quotations are taken from the New International Version (NIV). Copyright © 1985 by Zondervan Corporation.

Xulon Press
11350 Random Hills Road
Suite 800
Fairfax, VA 22030
(703) 279-6511
XulonPress.com

To order additional copies,
call 1-866-909-BOOK (2665)

CONTENTS

Acknowledgments

Dr. Thomas M. Thompson — thank you for instilling in me a love for Bible prophecy and for your invaluable contribution to this book.

To my wife, Teri — thank you for enriching my life and for your diligent efforts in preparing this book for publication. You are loved and appreciated.

Preface

I was a young man fresh out of college when a co-worker told me about his faith in Jesus Christ. Having had my fill of religion, I discounted his words... until he said to me, "You know, the Bible tells us that Jesus Christ is going to return to earth one day."

No, I didn't know that — had never heard anything about it. Then I was given a book that compared current events with what the Bible says will happen just before Jesus comes again. It blew my mind, and for the first time in my life I wanted to read and understand the Bible. I soon discovered the Old Testament had predicted in specific detail the birth, life, death, burial and resurrection of Jesus Christ. And then I studied what the Bible said about Jesus Christ coming again. I was amazed.

Shortly after making these discoveries, I surrendered my religion for a life-changing relationship with Jesus Christ. My life has not been the same since January 11, 1975, the day I trusted Jesus Christ as my Savior and Lord.

For almost thirty years now, I have continued to

look at our world, mindful of what the Bible says about the future. I have watched the signs or indicators increase and intensify over the past three decades. World events continue to point to the climax of human history as recorded in God's Word.

Over the years, I have sensed the Lord calling me to proclaim the truth that first brought me to the cross. On August 30, 2001, I told several friends who form the Board of our ministry that the Lord had impressed on my heart that we are heading for difficult and desperate times. A few days later, we faced the tragedy of September 11th. What I was sensing had become a stark reality.

In the months following 9/11, we have witnessed dramatic changes that have profoundly impacted our sense of security and well being. Each day's news is filled with updates on the war on terrorism. Alongside the daily pollen count, we hear the daily terrorist alert from the Office of Homeland Security. Events in the Middle East present us with the very real threat of a regional, if not global, war.

So what do we do? Learn more about Islam and try to figure out why they hate us? Act like nothing has happened and simply get back to the day-to-day tyranny of our lives? Let me offer a suggestion. Let's open up the Bible and see what it says about the future. And then let's look at what is happening in our world, especially since that dark September day, and make a comparison. I think you will be amazed and filled with hope. The parallel between *what is happening* in our world and what the Bible says *will happen* is absolutely incredible. God knows and controls the future and He has revealed it in the Bible. He has also told us that there *is* hope. Beyond the increasingly difficult days that are ahead, when the world seems destined to utter devastation, Jesus Christ will return and hope will become a glorious reality. Read on and see what I mean.

CHAPTER 1

WHY SEPTEMBER 11, 2001?

═══════════════════════════════════════

Fire, billows of smoke and unbelievable carnage . . . now they are seared into our personal and collective memories . . . and we have been changed. Like a physician probing an old, painful wound, each passing September 11 will bring back the piercing shock of that horrible day. We will remember the first flush of disbelief, the anger, and the sense of helplessness that overwhelmed us on *that* day. In our mind's eye, we will catch a glimpse of a demonic-looking face in the smoke rising from the World Trade Center's Twin Towers. Once again, that day's headlines will flash through our minds:

> Our Worst Day . . . Horror in the Sky . . .
> Day of Terror . . . Is This the End of the

World? . . . Day of Hell . . . Apocalypse
. . . Day That Changed the World

And again we will ask, Why? Why did it happen? Why would anyone do something so sick? Why do they hate us? And then there is the question we are almost reluctant to ask — Why didn't God stop those madmen?

To some Americans, September 11 is just a sign of religious extremism — a few fanatics carrying their beliefs too far. Others remember the celebrations and parties across the Arab and Muslim world on September 11. They see a clash of cultures, a conflict between two value systems that have trouble understanding and communicating with each other.

But more than this, September 11 was a wake-up call. It has awakened us to an all-out war against our way of life. Islamic fundamentalists like Osama bin Laden hate the American dream of personal freedom and responsibility. They want to compel everyone to submit to their religious beliefs.

Days after the terrorist attacks, former Israeli Prime Minister Benyamin "Bibi" Netanyahu was invited to make an address in Congress. Speaking out of his vast experience, as well as the personal loss of his own brother at the hands of terrorists, Netanyahu made his sentiments clear. He said, "We have received a wake-up call from hell. Now the question is simple. Do we rally to defeat this evil, while there is still time, or do we press a collective snooze button and go back to business as usual?" His answer was, "The time for action is now."[1]

SEPTEMBER 11 — A WAKE-UP CALL

When the alarm sounded and we were rudely awakened on the morning of September 11, we came face to face with a very harsh reality. We discovered we share this planet with people who hate us and, in the name of Allah, want to destroy us. These people are cold and calculating. They are willing to spend years in our country, living in our neighborhoods, shopping at our stores, studying in our schools, all the while looking for the opportunity to murder as many of us as possible. They do this believing they are doing the work of Allah. They are confident that upon death they will be rewarded by sensual pleasures in paradise.

The world holds over one billion Muslims. If even a small percentage of this one billion embraces radical Islamic beliefs, their numbers are staggering. In the ongoing battle against terrorism, the US has discovered that thousands of young men in their twenties and early thirties have been trained as terrorists in Osama bin Laden's camps. Despite our best efforts, the FBI and CIA estimate there could be a thousand terrorist "sleeper cells" in the United States today. We are at war, and the dangers around us are multiplying.

Converging Dangers

Five months after the September 11 attacks, CIA Director George J. Tenet appeared before the Senate Select Committee on Intelligence and spoke of the unique dangers we face in a post-9/11 world. Tenet's words were ominous:

> September 11 brought together and brought home — literally — several vital threats to the United States and its interests . . . It is the convergence of these threats that I want to emphasize with you today: the connection between terrorists and other enemies of this country; the weapons of mass destruction they seek to use against us; and the social, economic, and political tensions across the world that they exploit in mobilizing their followers.[2]

Notice Tenet's use of the term "convergence," which refers to two or more conditions or events coming together at essentially the same time. The weather in our home state of Texas often demonstrates the power that can be unleashed when multiple elements come together. When a cool front from the north converges with our torrid summer heat, together they can generate the destructive power of a fierce thunderstorm or tornado. Our country is facing a storm, too. Combine trained terrorists with rogue nations that sponsor terrorism, add in weapons of mass destruction, and what do we have? Unimaginable danger. Even Vice President Dick Cheney has gone on record, stating that it is only a matter of time before another "big event" occurs.

When we apply this concept of convergence to what the Bible says about the future, we reach the same conclusion. So many things are happening at the same time that fit what the Bible says about the future; we must be getting close to the very climax of history. Global changes in response to the war on terrorism are positioning our world for events predicted in the Bible. For example, the Jewish nation of Israel is in its land, struggling for peace. The Islamic world is becoming more and more hostile toward Israel. The European Union (EU), growing into a world power, is intervening to bring peace in the Middle East. All these trends represent exactly the conditions the Bible says will exist shortly before the return of Jesus Christ.

With George Tenet and others continuing to sound the alarm, it would seem that we have heard and heeded our wake-up call from hell. In part, we have. The US has certainly responded quickly and forcefully to the terrorist attacks. But for political reasons, we have understated the global threat of fundamentalist Islam. To avoid offending Muslim allies in the Middle East and peace loving Muslims across the globe, we have largely ignored a radical branch of their religious system that lies *behind* the attacks.

Islamic Extremists

Although mosques were proliferating across the nation, most Americans were largely ignorant of Islamic beliefs until the tragedy of September 11. My first exposure to the world of Islam came on a trip to Israel while Muslims were observing the fast of Ramadan. The day we went to the Wailing Wall has been etched into my memory. From a distance I saw the Wall, where devout Jews come to pray. Then I looked beyond the Wall and saw the Dome of the Rock. The sight moved me to tears. My mind raced through the biblical history of that sacred site. This is where Abraham was ready to offer up his son Isaac. This is where God's temple stood. This is where Jesus Christ taught, and in a moment of righteous anger, overturned the tables of the money-changers. And to this very spot Jesus Christ will one day return and bring peace to the earth.

The romance of the moment soon gave way to reality. Before we started up the ramp to the Temple Mount, our tour guide gave us several warnings. He told us the Palestinians might well ask us for money. If they did, we should refuse and leave. To gain access to the Mount, he suggested we hide our Bibles and walk in pairs rather than as one large group. He also warned us that if we stopped and appeared to be praying, we would be asked to leave.

One person in our group asked about actually going into the Dome of the Rock. Our guide shook his head in disgust, "I am not comfortable going in there." He went on to tell us that visitors are required to remove their shoes before entering the mosque and that at the entrance there is a sign that says something to this effect: "When you enter you are cursing the triune God."[3] Muslims vehemently reject the biblical truth that there is one God who has revealed Himself in three distinct Persons — the Father, the Son and the Holy Spirit. So just to visit this mosque, a Christian must deny a clear truth found in the Bible. How ironic, when we consider the Dome of the Rock adorns much of its interior walls with sayings from the life of Jesus Christ.

Islam rejects Christianity and Judaism. A significant segment of Islam's adherents devote their lives to compelling "the infidels" to submit to Allah. This attitude has produced the violence we have witnessed firsthand. But above all, Muslim fundamentalists are consumed by hatred for the Jews.

Most Americans are familiar with the deep animosity for Jews that prompts Palestinian suicide-homicide bombers to target innocent Israeli citizens. Among the ordinary Palestinian population, these men and women become instant heroes. Posters featuring their faces are plastered throughout their communities. Huge murals glorify their "heroic" terrorist acts, graphically depicting the mangled bodies of dead and dying Jews. Palestinian community leaders have even gone to the expense of building huge models of the buildings their followers have destroyed. They encourage their people to walk inside these models and celebrate the "martyrs" who caused the death of their Jewish enemies.

But it is not just the September 11 terrorists and the Palestinians who hate God's chosen people. America's Arab allies, the "moderate" members of the Muslim establishment, often express the same sentiments. The Muslim cleric Shaikh Saad Al-Buraik, for example, has connections to the ruling family in Saudi Arabia. In a two-day telethon that raised over $100 million for the Palestinian cause, he called Jews "monkeys" and called on Muslims to enslave Jewish women. This Muslim clergyman believes the Palestinians have been too mild in their treatment of the Jews. His words are filled with hatred: "Muslim Brothers in Palestine, do not have any mercy or compassion on the Jews, their blood, their money, their flesh. Their women are yours to take, legitimately. Allah made them yours. Why don't you enslave their women? Why don't you wage *jihad* [holy war]? Why don't you pillage them?"[4]

Most Muslims would never dream of personally launching an attack on America or Israel. But many Muslims have a deep sympathy for the values and goals of Islamic extremists and are willing to contribute money to their organizations. Even the Westernized, English-speaking Muslims of Great Britain often echo the viewpoint of America's terrorist enemies. In a November 2001 opinion poll, four out of five of them believed that the anti-terrorist military action by the US and Britain in Afghanistan was unjustified. Most of them considered the war on terrorism a war against Islam, their religion.[5] Commentator Tony Blankely has stated it well: "So long as the Arab masses live in hope of triumphant Islam, the West will live in fear of terror."[6]

SEPTEMBER 11 — A WARNING

Since 9/11, we have been bombarded by constant warnings about terrorist attacks in America and Europe. Will they go away? US Homeland Security

Director Tom Ridge emphatically says, "No." Speaking seven months after the September 11 attacks, he reported that Osama bin Laden's al Qaeda terrorists were trying to acquire nuclear weapons and could be counted on to try to use them if they got their hands on them. "The world is just as dangerous today, if not more so. The threat is real; it's as real as it was seven months ago," he warned. "In fact, it is a permanent condition to which this country must permanently adapt."[7]

Let's think about Ridge's comments for a moment. The threat of terrorism in America is permanent. We will never again feel totally secure.

The Bible also gives us a warning of disasters ahead. In fact, let me be a reluctant "prophet" and describe what is coming. Violence, corruption, abuse, and outright hatred will flourish and actually seem to be winning the battle against order and justice. "There will be terrible times (or times of terror!) in the last days," the Bible says, and goes on to describe a chaotic and oppressive time much like our own.[8] I'm afraid that's what we can expect in the days to come. More of the same . . . only worse. God's Word even anticipates more men like Osama bin Laden. They are described as abusive, treacherous men who are full of their own piety, yet completely out of touch with genuine spiritual power. Instead, they will turn to the kind of power they understand — the power of force.

As we get closer and closer to what the Bible calls, "the end of the age," man's evil will be evident; and God will begin to judge this world. There will be earthquakes, famines, disease, massive death and global destruction. The horror of 9/11 was a preview of things to come.

SEPTEMBER 11 — A STAGE-SETTER

When Bibi Netanyahu presented his testimony before the United States Congress, he said, "What is at stake today is nothing less than the survival of our civilization. There may be some who would have thought a week ago that to talk in these apocalyptic terms about the battle against international terrorism was to engage in reckless exaggeration. No longer."[9] No one challenged Netanyahu's words. In fact, he received an overwhelming ovation. Why? Because we know he is right.

The survival of our civilization *is* in the balance, just as Netanyahu stated.

So, are we seeing the final act on the stage of modern civilization? God's Word has already scripted the events that will take place.

The Bible and the Future

The Bible says that as we come closer and closer to the climax of history, Israel will be center-stage on the international scene. Have you watched the news lately?

The Bible clearly teaches that the final act begins with Israel entering into a peace agreement. The signing of this agreement will not bring lasting peace, but will open the door to a time of utter destruction. Today, the pursuit of peace in the Middle East dominates the international scene.

The Bible also tells us that a major world power will re-emerge and will be instrumental in negotiating the coming peace agreement in the Middle East. That world power is a revived form of the ancient Roman Empire. Today, the European Union looks a lot like a new version of the old Roman Empire, and the EU is currently taking a more prominent role in the Middle East crisis.

The Bible says the closing act will include utter devastation and death. We have now been alerted to the possible use of weapons of mass destruction, even in these United States. Could these weapons be part of the destruction described in the Bible? Do these weapons preview things to come?

As we have seen, 9/11 was a wake-up call. It has alerted us to converging events that point to the return of Jesus Christ. 9/11 was also a warning, a preview of events the Bible says are soon to come. But above all, the events of 9/11 have actually accelerated worldwide changes that signal the approaching climax of history.

This is an incredible time to be alive. Even those who do not accept the Bible as the Word of God are using biblical terms to describe what is happening around us. The wake-up call on 9/11 sent shockwaves throughout the world. They continue to reverberate even months later. In our collective consciousness we know that something is going on ... and we sense that something is going to happen. The Bible actually tells us what lies ahead. In fact, over twenty-five hundred years ago a Hebrew prophet, living in what is now the land of Iraq, predicted that a peace agreement between Israel and her Arab neighbors would begin the final countdown.

Chapter One Endnotes

[1]"Statement of former Israeli Prime Minister Benyamin Netanyahu before the Committee on Government Reform of the United States House of Representatives, September 20, 2001" (http://www.house. gov/reform/statement_of_netanyahu.htm; retrieved June 4, 2002).

[2]"Worldwide Threat — Converging Dangers in a Post 9/11 World," Testimony of Director of Central Intelligence George J. Tenet before the Senate Select Committee on Intelligence, February 6, 2002 (http://www.cia.gov/cia/public_affairs/speeches/dci_speech_0206200 2.html; retrieved June 4, 2002).

[3]See Lambert Dolphin, "Allah and the Temple Mount" (http://www. templemount.org/allah.html, retrieved June 4, 2002).

[4]See "Saudi Telethon Host Calls for Enslaving Jewish Women," National Review, April 26, 2002 (http://www.nationalreview.com/document/document042602.asp; retrieved June 4, 2002).

[5]"ICM Research/Today: Muslims Poll, November 2001," http://www. icmresearch.co.uk/reviews/2001/today-muslims-poll-nov-2001.htm; retrieved June 4, 2002).

[6]Tony Blankley, "Darkness is Better for Illusions," *The Washington Times*, May 1, 2002 (http://www.washtimes.com/op-ed/20020501-81109227.htm; retrieved June 4, 2002).

[7]Ron Fournier, "Ridge Says Terrorism is Permanent," *Washington Post* (http://www.washingtonpost.com/ac2/wp-dyn/A3665-2002 Apr29?language=printer; retrieved May 9, 2002).

[8]2 Timothy 3:1-8.

[9]"Statement of former Israeli Prime Minister Benyamin Netanyahu."

CHAPTER 2

THE COMING
MIDDLE EAST PEACE

A n incredible fact — a peace agreement in the Middle East will begin a seven-year countdown to the return of Christ. Today, the war on terrorism has brought overwhelming pressure on Israel to enter into just such an agreement.

THE BIBLE AND TODAY'S NEWS

Open your newspaper. What do you read? "Suicide Bomber Kills Fifteen at Tel Aviv Restaurant." "Israeli Occupation Blamed for Terrorist Attack." "Arab Leaders Denounce Israel."

Turn on your television and check out the news. What do you see? "Crisis in the Middle East." "War on Terror." "Mideast Turmoil."

Many of us have grown weary of the never-ending tension. Since 9/11, it has become especially intense . . . and there seems to be no solution in sight. Will it ever end? You and I may be experiencing Middle East fatigue. But I suspect that, if the prophet Daniel were alive today rather than 2,500 years ago, he would be watching CNN, MSNBC, and FOX News — nodding and saying, "This is what Gabriel *told* me would happen!"

DANIEL IN THE LAND OF SADDAM HUSSEIN

When Daniel wrote of a future peace, he lived in a large empire north of Israel called Babylon. Today, we know that land as Iraq. In Daniel's time, King Nebuchadnezzar was the great Mideast troublemaker. Today Dictator Saddam Hussein rules with an iron hand.

In the sixth century BC, Nebuchadnezzar did what Saddam Hussein would like to do. He handily defeated the Jews and ravaged the city of Jerusalem and its temple. He deported many Jews, including a boy named Daniel, from Jerusalem to Babylon. Long before he spent a night in a den of lions, Daniel was thrown into a den of idol-worshippers. Nebuchadnezzar's troops carried him off to Babylon, a country that had no respect for the God of Israel.

Daniel lived the rest of his life in the Babylonian Empire. He was taken there as a teenager, but still held fast to his faith in God while living in this pagan land. His God-given ability to interpret dreams and foretell the future earned him an important position in the Babylonian government. And when he was a very old man, the Lord sent the angel Gabriel to give him, and us, a look at the future for Israel and the world.

THE DEATH OF THE MESSIAH

Although he wrote more than five hundred years before Jesus Christ was born, Daniel recorded for us when Jesus would be born, why He would come, and how His people would reject him. This prophecy is so miraculous that many skeptics would like to explain it away. They'd like to declare it a forgery written years *after* Jesus came to earth. But that won't work. We have ancient copies of Daniel's prophecy that were transcribed long *before* Jesus was born.

In response to Daniel's heartfelt prayers for his people, God sent the angel Gabriel to Daniel to tell him what the future would hold for the Jews. The future of Israel would be divided into two distinct time periods. The first time period would begin with an order or decree to rebuild the city of Jerusalem. This same time period would end with the promised Messiah being rejected by His own people. We know when this decree was issued. When we calculate the amount of time specified in this prophecy we arrive at the actual time when Jesus was crucified.

When Jesus was rejected by his people, the first half of Daniel's prophecy was fulfilled.

The angel Gabriel told Daniel that Israel's promised Messiah would come and be rejected by his people. He said this would occur in a period of time that would begin with a decree to rebuild the city of Jerusalem. Over four hundred years before Christ was born, in the Jewish month of Nisan during the twentieth year of his reign, Artaxerxes Longimanus issued that order or decree.[1] Following the Jewish calendar, we can calculate Daniel's prediction and determine a specific date. Putting Artaxerxes' decree at March 5, 444 BC, we arrive at the exact year — even the exact *day* — when Jesus presented himself to Israel as Messiah. That was March 30, 33 AD, the day of his Triumphal Entry into Jerusalem. We commemorate that Triumphal Entry on Palm Sunday. Immediately afterward, he was "cut off" by crucifixion . . . just as Daniel had foretold.[2]

With Israel's rejection of her Messiah, the first part of Daniel's prophecy was fulfilled. The second part of Daniel's prophecy, a period of just seven years, is still future. Therefore, seven years remain in God's plan for the nation of Israel to become once again the center of world events as predicted by Daniel. When will this countdown begin? It will begin with a Middle East peace agreement between Israel and her neighbors.

PEACE IN THE MIDDLE EAST

Remember, Daniel recorded this prophecy 2,500 years ago. How could he have predicted what we are seeing play out right in front of our eyes? Consider for a moment what must be in place in order for Daniel's final seven-year countdown to begin. First of all, Daniel's nation, Israel, must be established in its homeland before it can enter into a peace agreement. Israel did not have a land of its own from 70 AD until the year 1948. During this time a remnant of Jewish people did remain in the land. However, for almost 2,000 years, a huge majority of Jews (or Israelites) were dispersed in various lands around the world. The Bible predicted this scattering of the Jews as divine punishment for their disobedience (Leviticus 23).

In addition to Israel's existence as a nation, there must be an urgent need for a peace agreement. Today, Israel is surrounded by Arab and Muslim nations, many of whom are bent on its destruction. Israel's enemies have increased their efforts to destroy this tiny nation. Because of its precarious position as such a small and vulnerable nation, Israel's desire for peace has dominated the country's entire culture. The major world powers, including the United States and Europe, strive daily for stability in the Middle East. They want nothing less than a permanent peace in the Middle East. The push for peace is on.

THE TEMPLE WILL BE REBUILT

Daniel's prophecy of a future peace agreement strongly suggests there will be a provision or a plan for rebuilding Israel's temple. The angel Gabriel told Daniel that three-and-a-half years after this peace agreement is signed, the leader who negotiates the peace agreement will turn against Israel. He will then halt sacrifices in the Hebrew temple and desecrate or dishonor the temple itself.

In order for this to happen, the city of Jerusalem and the Temple Mount must be under Israel's control. After almost two thousand years, Israel finally took back the city and the Temple Mount during its Six Day War with Egypt and other Arab nations in 1967. Now the stage is set for the rebuilding of the temple and the resumption of the sacrifices in the temple.

Rebuilding the temple is not like throwing together an office building. How will the builders know what architectural design to follow? Where do we find the blueprints for a structure that was destroyed two thousand years ago? The barriers to construction might seem insurmountable, but Israeli groups like the "Temple Mount Faithful" and the "Temple Institute" have dedicated their efforts to rebuilding this yet-future Jewish temple. Diagrams have been drawn and the actual temple could be completely rebuilt in as little as nine months.

What about the priests in this temple? Where are the special garments they must wear? Where are the ritual vessels and sacred implements to be used in their sacrifices? Garments have already been woven and sacrificial instruments are in existence, ready to use.

It is worth noting that only descendants of Moses' brother Aaron qualify for this Jewish priesthood. After the passing of more than two thousand years, who is there that can prove his authentic lineage *now*? Aaron's family has been submerged among the Jewish people for centuries. But scientists have discovered a unique DNA marker they have called the "Cohen gene," providing a possible high-tech method to pinpoint Aaron's descendants.[3]

How will this new temple be dedicated to God again? The Old Testament prescribes that a *red heifer* must be offered up to initiate the sacrificial system, which God personally gave to Moses. There is just one hitch. From ancient times, until the modern state of Israel was founded, there were no red heifers in Israel. But as recently as April 2002, a red heifer was born in Israel. Some rabbis believe this animal could be the perfect red heifer needed to resume the sacrificial system in the temple.

Finally, opinion polls reveal that plans to rebuild the temple and offer blood sacrifices are growing more popular in Israel. Ultra-orthodox Jews are gaining political power, in part because many recent immigrants from Eastern Europe are embracing strict traditional Judaism. The idea of rebuilding the temple used to sound preposterous even to many Israelis. Not any more.

It was September 28, 2000, when Ariel Sharon, accompanied by over 1,000 Israeli police officers, made his way past the Wailing Wall up the ramp to the Temple Mount. The Palestinians responded to Sharon's thirty-four-minute visit with violence that continues to this day. They call their opposition the "al-Aqsa intifida." Muslims have even renamed the Temple Mount, Judaism's holiest place, and refer to it as Haram al-Sharif. The search for peace may well include some agreement allowing Jews, Muslims and Christians to share this sacred soil.

The international community longs for peace in the Middle East. As news reports testify daily, Israel desperately yearns for peace. How much longer will it take? Will there soon be a peace agreement that fulfills Daniel's ancient prophecy?

ISRAEL'S QUEST FOR PEACE

Since its formation in 1948, Israel has sought peace with its hostile Arab and Muslim neighbors. Its efforts have seldom paid off, but Israel has never given up. And as militant fundamentalist Islam has hardened its terror-driven stance toward Israel, the Jewish nation has become more and more desperate for peace. Israel has offered more to its Arab enemies while expecting fewer concessions from them:

- Israel was an infant nation of just 717,000 Jews when it was attacked in 1948 by six hostile Arab neighbors that vastly outnumbered it. Miraculously, Israel survived.
- In the 1956 Suez Military Campaign, Israel captured the Sinai Desert peninsula. But what Israel really wanted was peace, not more territory. Israel willingly withdrew its troops in deference to UN peacekeeping forces, hoping that peace could be achieved with Egypt.
- In the 1967 Six-Day War, Israel gained control of Jerusalem, Judea, Samaria, and Sinai, which it had returned to Egypt in 1956. Frustrated in their attacks against Israel, Palestinians began terrorist attacks against the Jews in Israel and

around the world.

- In the 1973 Yom Kippur War, Israel accepted a cease-fire and withdrew its troops from captured territories just as it was poised for victory. Israel wanted peace, not more land.
- In 1979, in exchange for peace, Israel returned over 90% of the land it had won from Egypt. It was then that Israeli Prime Minister Begin shared the Nobel Peace Prize with Egyptian President Anwar Sadat.
- In the 1987-93 Palestinian uprising, stone-throwing teenagers were egged on to attack the Israeli army. Meanwhile, Israel proposed a peace process like the one later accepted in the "Oslo Accords" in the capital city of Norway.
- In 1993, Israel signed the Oslo Accords, which included Israel handing a great deal of territory over to Yasser Arafat's Palestinian Liberation Organization. Arafat founded the PLO in 1964 with the aim of destroying Israel completely. Israel gave up land for peace, but received no peace in return.

In the Oslo agreement, Yasser Arafat promised to renounce terrorism. Israel, in exchange, would accept a Palestinian state. Arafat did not keep his promise. His Palestinian Authority, established by the Oslo Accords, has continued to finance, organize and encourage terrorist activities. Tensions continue to mount daily. Something has to give!

Even as Yasser Arafat has continued to make war, Israel's leaders have tried to forge a lasting peace.

Former Israeli Prime Minister Ehud Barak proposed giving much of eastern Jerusalem to a future Palestinian State. This concession outraged millions of Israelis, including peace activist Leah Rabin, a personal friend of Yasser Arafat and his wife. Leah is the widow of Israeli Prime Minister Yitzhak Rabin, who signed the Oslo Accords with Yasser Arafat, accompanied by many handshakes. An Israeli opponent of his peace efforts assassinated Mr. Rabin. "Yitzhak is spinning in his grave!" Mrs. Rabin said of Israel's proposed giveaway to the PLO. But Barak's gift of eastern Jerusalem was still not enough for Arafat . . . the peace process fizzled. A few months later, faced with the spectacular failure of Barak's peace efforts, Israeli voters elected the more hard-line Ariel Sharon as Prime Minister.

Since Sharon's election, the Palestinians' attacks on Israel have increased. Prime Minister Sharon, undeterred, has pursued Israel's efforts for peace. Despite finding hard proof that Yasser Arafat is still ordering his troops to murder Israeli citizens, Sharon continues to offer Arafat and the Palestinians their own territory and nationhood. Rejecting the conservative policies of his own political party, he asks only that Arafat stop his attacks on Israel, including the famous homicide-bomber attacks that specially target even helpless children and families. Arafat has responded with friendly words — accompanied by vicious deeds.

Currently, Israel's population stands at less than six million Jews. Ninety million Arabs surround Israel's immediate borders. And there are as many as

1.6 billion Muslims across the world. Many of these Arabs and Muslims eagerly look forward to a day when Israel is pushed into the sea. For the sake of peace, Israel is willing to give up hard-won land that it needs for its own defense. Israel is ready to allow the creation of a state that may be controlled by the Palestinian terrorists who have been attacking innocent Israeli citizens all along. There are many Palestinians who do not want peace. Their prayer to Allah is that Israel will be destroyed forever.

THE PRESSURE FOR PEACE

Today it may seem as though Israel's half-century quest for peace has ultimately failed. However, since 9/11, it is not just Israel who desires peace in the Middle East. The United States and Europe also want a permanent Mideast peace. They need peace so that their war on terrorism can move ahead smoothly. They need peace so oil, the life-blood of their economies, will continue to flow to them from the Middle East. And the US has wanted peace in the Middle East so it can safely take down Saddam Hussein, one of the greatest threats to world stability.

The early successes of America's war on terrorism have come from the US's high-tech weaponry — and the cooperation of Muslim nations like Pakistan and Saudi Arabia. These countries are unusual allies in a war against Muslim terrorists. Saudi Arabia is a rich spawning ground for Islamic terrorists. Osama bin Laden was born in Saudi Arabia, as were many of his 9/11 attackers. Before the terrorist attacks,

Pakistan was the outside world's strongest supporter of the pro-terrorist Taliban regime in Afghanistan. Terrorists continue to find most of their recruits from strongly Muslim societies like Saudi Arabia and Pakistan.

Many citizens of Muslim countries like Pakistan and Saudi Arabia deeply resent the nation of Israel. Saudi Arabia has, for now, joined America in fighting Muslim terrorism. But it also gives rewards to the families of the Palestinian homicide bombers who blow up Israel's innocents in restaurants, at bus stops and in other public places. As long as the fighting between Israel and the Palestinians continues, the Saudis will keep asking themselves, "Why are we siding with America, when she is Israel's greatest supporter?" To keep their anti-terror coalition together, the US and its European allies need to calm the situation. Peace in the Middle East will benefit everyone.

The United States and Europe also need peace in order to fuel their economies. The world's top five oil-rich nations have Muslim governments and an overwhelming number of Muslim citizens. This top-five nation list includes the hard-line Islamic countries of Saudi Arabia and Iran, along with Mideast troublemaker Iraq.[4] In 1973, the world caught a glimpse of what could happen if these nations decided to close the oil spigot. That year, the oil-exporting nations flexed their muscle with an embargo. As long lines formed at America's gasoline stations, oil prices skyrocketed to levels previously thought impossible. At the end of that traumatic year, the President announced that because of the energy crisis, even the lights on the national Christmas tree in Washington, D.C. would not be lit.

That was over a quarter-century ago, but the balance of world power has not been the same since. The Administrator of the Energy Information Administration has said that 1973 was in some ways "the most pivotal year in energy history."[5]

In April of 2002, Iraqi dictator Saddam Hussein tried a rerun of 1973. In retaliation for Israeli actions toward the Palestinians, he announced a shutoff of Iraqi oil to Israel and to the US, Israel's main ally.[6] Saddam's scheme didn't work, because other Arab and Muslim nations did not join his embargo. But next time, we may not be so lucky. Both the US and Europe need Arab oil. To keep that oil flowing, peace in the Middle East is a prerequisite.

Saddam Hussein's 2002 oil cutoff is just one example of his efforts to upset the stability of the Middle East. In 1990, he greedily gobbled up his oil-rich neighbor, Kuwait. Israel remained aloof in the resulting Persian Gulf War, but Saddam lobbed missiles at tiny Israel anyway. As always, Saddam aimed to stir up trouble. He has spent billions of dollars developing weapons of mass destruction. He has produced anthrax, botulinum toxin, and other deadly biological weapons. He has employed lethal chemicals against Iran and even against his own people, making Iraq one of the few nations to use these gruesome weapons in recent history. Saddam Hussein has also labored hard to possess a nuclear capability. In the early 1980's, Israel dealt his nuclear plans a major blow when it bombed his Osirak nuclear reactor. But Saddam's nuclear program has resumed vigorously.

America is anxious to stop Saddam Hussein from playing with matches on top of the Mideast powder keg. But it will be difficult and dangerous to remove Saddam without the support of Iraq's Arab and Muslim neighbors. The turmoil between Israel and the Palestinians at present blocks that support. Once again, Israel is the issue. To get a clear shot at Saddam Hussein, the US needs peace between Israel and its neighbors.

Amazing, isn't it? Twenty-five hundred years ago Daniel predicted that a peace agreement in the Middle East would begin the last seven years of God's plan for the nation of Israel and the nations that surround her. Humanly speaking, Israel should have long since ceased to exist as a people. Every day that Israel continues to occupy center stage on the international scene brings us one day closer to the peace agreement predicted by the prophet Daniel. Each day that passes is also an opportunity to present a spiritual wake-up call to a needy world. If the struggle for peace in the Middle East continues for another fifty plus years, it will only be because God is graciously extending an invitation to come to the cross before the countdown begins.

So peace in the Middle East has suddenly become a top priority not only for Israel, but for Europe and America, as well. With a population of only six million, Israel needs the support of these great powers. Under US and European pressure, Israel has already agreed to carve out a national land for the Palestinians. As the pressure steadily increases, the day will come when a definitive treaty is signed. Could it be the treaty Daniel predicted?

A peace treaty is on its way . . . the war on terrorism is demanding it. When it comes, few will suspect how temporary that peace will be. In reality, this peace agreement will launch the seven-year period that the Bible calls the tribulation. Today's war on terrorism is already positioning our world for events that we know will take place during the tribulation period. After a couple of years of relative peace, the world will enter a time of global devastation. It will be the real Apocalypse . . . a level of destruction that seemed unimaginable until July 16, 1945 . . . the day the world's first atomic bomb was tested. The war on terrorism has alerted us to the possibility of a nuclear disaster. Does the Bible predict the use of these weapons? Read on.

Chapter Two Endnotes

[1] See Nehemiah 2:1-9.

[2] Daniel 9:24-27 identifies three time periods. The first period, lasting 49 years, presumably refers to the time it took to complete the rebuilding of Jerusalem. After 434 years more, "the Anointed One will be cut off and will have nothing" (Daniel 7:26). Together, these two time periods add up to 483 years (49 years plus 434 years).

Using our modern Gregorian calendar, the period from Artaxerxes' decree to Jesus' Triumphal Entry takes up 476 years. But Gabriel's prophecy seems to rely upon a Jewish calendar of twelve thirty-day months (see Genesis 7:11, 24; 8:3-4; compare Revelation 11:2 with Revelation 11:3). Using this Hebrew calendar, *exactly* 483 years separate March 5, 444 BC, the probable date of Artaxerxes' decree, from March 30, AD 33, the day of Jesus' Triumphal Entry.

The third time period mentioned in Daniel 9 is the seven-year tribulation period, which is still to come. For further explanation, see the Web site www.johnonline.org.

[3] Yaakov Kleiman, "The Discovery of the 'Cohen Gene,'" *Jewish Action*, winter 1999 (http://www.ou.org/publications/ja/5760winter/cohen%20gene.pdf; retrieved June 4, 2002).

[4] "Greatest Oil Reserves by Country, 2001," infoplease.com (http://www.infoplease.com/ipa/A0872964.html; retrieved June 4, 2002).

[5] "25th Anniversary of the 1973 Oil Embargo," The Energy Information Administration (http://www.eia.doe.gov/emeu/25opec/anniversary.html; retrieved June 4, 2002).

[6] "Saddam Announces Oil Stoppage: Text," BBC News (http://news.bbc.co.uk/hi/english/world/monitoring/media_reports/newsid_1917000/1917361.stm; retrieved June 4, 2002)

CHAPTER 3

NUKES IN THE NEIGHBORHOOD

We've seen it repeatedly . . . in films, history books, even cartoons and television ads. "It" is the atomic mushroom cloud, one of the most recognizable images of our time. Even children understand it. No one has to explain. But what if you had just seen a nuclear explosion for the first time? How would you describe it? How about this . . . "The sky receded like a scroll, rolling up."

These words were written almost two thousand years ago by the apostle John and are recorded in the sixth chapter of the book of Revelation. John is writing about a yet future incident in the all-consuming wars and judgments just before Jesus comes again.

Outside the prophetic vision recorded in the book of Revelation, John never viewed a mushroom cloud. His age could not imagine wars with casualty rates climbing into the tens of millions. Gunpowder was unknown. Muscles, not explosives, overcame the enemy. And no weapon existed that could kill more than a few people at one time. A wild winter storm was perhaps the closest thing John had ever seen to the sky-curdling scene he described. Yet his image of the mushroom cloud was photographically precise. Commentator Henry Swete, himself writing in 1911, years before the creation of nuclear weapons, said the "exact sense" of John's words is that "the expanse of heaven . . . was seen to crack and part, the divided portions curling up and forming a roll on either hand"[1] — just like the two rolls at the head of a nuclear mushroom cloud.

In his vision, John says, the sun turned black like goat's-hair sackcloth, while the entire moon turned red. These words could be describing atmospheric disturbances caused by a nuclear detonation. Consider author Jonathan Schell's description of the atmospheric effects of even a relatively small one-megaton nuclear explosion: "as the mushroom cloud rushed overhead . . . the light from the sun would be blotted out, and day would turn to night."[2] John tells us he also saw the stars in the sky fall to earth, as late figs drop from a fig tree when it is shaken by a strong wind. There are those who suggest these could be missiles blazing earthward from space. In the ancient world, bright objects in the sky — like comets and meteors — were called stars.

THE ELEMENTS DESTROYED BY FIRE

In another New Testament passage,[3] the apostle Peter describes the coming destruction of the earth.

The day of destruction, he tells us, will come suddenly, like a thief. Peter is not writing about overpopulation, global warming, pollution, or some other hazard that might, over a period of decades or centuries, gradually make earth less livable. As serious as these issues may be, they will not suddenly destroy our planet. The Bible predicts that the end of modern civilization will come with breathtaking suddenness. And if human actions do play a part, they will be the swift and crippling blows of warfare conducted with WMD's — weapons of mass destruction.

Peter continues, telling us the heavens will disappear *with a roar*. The book *Nuclear War Survival Skills*, published by the US government's Oak Ridge National Laboratory, reads like a commentary on Peter's account. It explains the impact of the smallscale beginning stages of a nuclear war, describing the disappearance of the entire skyline into the blinding light of nuclear fireballs, even hundreds of miles from the points of detonation. At the same time, these bombs would generate a tremendous roar, audible across a continent: "The thunderous booms of the initial SLBM explosions would be heard over almost all parts of the United States. Persons one hundred miles away from a nuclear explosion may receive their first warning by hearing it about 7-1/2 minutes later."[4]

Next, Peter says, the elements will be destroyed by fire, and the earth and everything in it will be laid bare. What type of fire can *destroy* the elements? Decades ago, evangelist Billy Graham said, "When the prophets speak of fire in the world's judgment, or when Peter mentions fire at the end of the age, it is not likely that they refer to the fire of combustion. It could be the fire of fission, the release of nuclear power by the splitting of the atom."[5]

To the twenty-first-century eye, Peter's apocalyptic vision may seem drearily familiar. It may conjure images of "B" grade end-of-the-world movies. But in Peter's time, the collapse of a tower in the community of Siloam that resulted in eighteen fatalities would be screaming-headline news. The idea of a firestorm capable of consuming the entire earth was a concept alien to his experience. It is nothing short of astonishing that Peter can express so clearly the idea that the coming fire will not only destroy the entire world, but will cause the dissolution of the very elements, the building blocks of matter.

Can you imagine anyone — ancient or modern — painting a more vivid picture of nuclear destruction than the one given to us by the apostles John and Peter? And since September 11, 2001, we live in a world that seems to be determined to bring such a holocaust to pass.

How did things get this bad?

THE BIRTH OF THE BOMB

It all started at the Trinity test site near Alamogordo, New Mexico, on the morning of July 16, 1945. The scientists gathered there didn't set out to rewrite the dictionary. They were trying to win a world war. They had built a new weapon, and they wanted to know if it worked.

It worked. At 5:49 a.m. on that rain-soaked morning, the world's first atomic bomb was detonated.[6] The sky ignited into a yellow-red fireball rising eight miles above the earth, transforming the pre-dawn darkness into a blinding, searing flame that turned night into day for over a hundred miles.[7] Twenty miles away, physicist Enrico Fermi felt the bomb's blast wave.[8]

The test bomb detonated at Alamogordo was a mere toy by later standards. The *Tsar Bomba*, built by the Soviet Union, was *five thousand* times more powerful.[9] But the scientists who gathered to witness the explosion already recognized the massive fatalities that nuclear weapons could inflict. They understood that such devices could rain invisible destruction upon people hundreds of miles away. They realized that nuclear explosions could even decompose the very elements that make up the planet.

In short, they knew they had learned how to destroy the world. Dr. J. Robert Oppenheimer, the flamboyant scientific director of the nuclear-bomb project, recalled a line from the Hindu Scriptures: "I am become death, the shatterer of worlds!"[10] Explosives expert Dr. George B. Kistiakowsky was more down-to-earth, but his reaction was similar: "I am sure that at the end of the world, in the last millisecond of earth's existence, the last human will see what we saw."[11]

Before 1945, people did not think of earthly weaponry when they read the judgments recorded in biblical prophecies. No human weapons could match the scope and destructive power of the biblical plagues. But since then, we have found it more and more difficult to read prophecy *without* envisioning modern warfare.

The Bomb has made the difference. In the 1933 edition of the 16,000-page *Oxford English Dictionary*, the definition of "apocalypse," another name for the book of Revelation, has nothing to do with war or destruction. But today, reporters and pundits routinely use this term to refer to the threat of massive nuclear conflict and to the kind of devastating terrorist attack that the US witnessed on September 11, 2001. They automatically connect the immense destruction that humans can now inflict upon one another with the word *apocalypse* — the Greek name of the book of Revelation.

Today millions of Americans, as they read the Bible, find seemingly endless parallels between the world in which they live and the world painted in prophecy. In the 1980's, President Reagan remarked, "You know, I turn back to your ancient prophets in the Old Testament and the signs foretelling Armageddon, and I find myself considering if we're the generation that is going to see that come about. I don't know if you noted any of those prophecies lately but, believe me, they certainly describe the times we're going through."[12]

Since the terrorist attacks on New York and Washington and Flight 93, matters are even worse. The biblical images shadow our daily lives more than ever. What we used to fear because it was *pos-*

sible, we now see actually beginning to happen around us. Since the 1940's, nuclear weapons have given us the ability to inflict on our planet the devastation described in Revelation. But the nations that originally built those weapons did so in fear. They knew that any nuclear exchange could easily escalate into an all-engulfing war that might destroy civilization. *Everyone* would lose. Today's Islamic terrorists, on the other hand, think they *cannot* lose. They gleefully dish out whatever banquet of death they can cook up, confident that Allah will bring their cause to ultimate victory. And they have shown a strong taste for nuclear weapons.

FALSE ALARM

Days after 9/11, a US intelligence report indicated terrorists had obtained a ten-kiloton nuclear weapon and planned to smuggle it into New York City. At first the information was not given to President Bush. When he was finally informed, he immediately ordered his national security team to make it their number-one priority to counter the threat of nuclear terrorism. His concern was understandable. If the report was accurate, the nation's largest and most crowded city would soon be threatened by a weapon of frighteningly destructive power. This compact, inconspicuous package would be two-thirds as powerful as the atom bomb that devastated the city of Hiroshima in 1945. At that time, the initial explosion instantly killed tens of thousands of Japanese civilians. The final death toll was in the hundreds of thousands.

The warning President Bush received in the last week of October 2001 was a false alarm. New York City still stands. But that does not mean that US leaders are "breathing easy." Government investigators have examined the evidence that such a bomb was headed for New York. They have found that it could be relatively easy for Osama bin Laden's al Qaeda organization or another terrorist group to obtain nuclear weapons. It is sobering to observe how much progress the terrorists have already made toward grasping the nuclear trigger:

- Osama bin Laden has boasted that he already has nuclear and chemical weapons.[13] A senior member of al Qaeda's command is reported to have boasted, "there will be another attack and it's going to be much bigger" than what happened on September 11, 2001.
- In October 2001, Pakistani officials arrested two nuclear scientists and questioned them about their contacts with Osama bin Laden and al Qaeda. Both scientists have been released, though one of them has repeatedly failed polygraph tests.
- Russia has decommissioned about *ten thousand* tactical nuclear weapons since 1991, but it has been able to document the whereabouts of only a small portion of that inventory.
- In 1996, the late Russian General Alexander Lebed claimed that his government had lost 134 mini-nukes, each compact enough to fit

into a small suitcase. And reports have surfaced that Osama Laden bought twenty of them for $30 million, plus two tons of opium.[14]

- In the late 1990's, Afghan and Pakistani smugglers were bringing so much nuclear material out of the former Soviet Union that they had to find a warehouse in which to store it.
- Russia's internal-security agencies report that on hundreds of occasions they have seized nuclear materials or technical documents that have fallen into the wrong hands.
- The United Nations' International Atomic Energy Agency has reported 175 cases of trafficking in nuclear materials since 1993.

The Bush administration is alarmed by the growing evidence of al Qaeda's progress toward obtaining nuclear bombs or easy-to-make dirty nuclear devices, which use a dynamite charge or other conventional explosives to scatter radioactive materials. The government has deployed hundreds of sophisticated radiation sensors at US borders, overseas outposts, and central locations around the nation's capital. America's elite commando unit, the Delta Force, remains on a standby alert to seize control of any nuclear materials the sensors may detect. Cabinet members have participated in exercises to identify the life-and-death choices the President will have to make if the new sensors detect significant radiation on a boat cruising up the Potomac River, for example, or a vehicle traveling on I-95 toward the United States Capitol. The new concern regarding nuclear dangers explains President Bush's secret decision to activate a "shadow government" of senior federal managers in underground bunkers outside of Washington. No other President since the beginning of the nuclear age has been compelled to take such action.

Officials in Washington are not alone in their appraisal of the new nuclear threat. As they survey the post-September military landscape, nuclear scientists are also deeply concerned about the likelihood of nuclear terrorism. If we think of our world as a clock, with the stroke of twelve as the moment when the earth explodes in a major nuclear conflict, it's clear — we are moving closer and closer to midnight.

CLOSER TO MIDNIGHT

Next to the mushroom cloud, the best-known symbol of the nuclear age is probably the Doomsday Clock of the *Bulletin of the Atomic Scientists*. This imaginary clock, set at seven minutes to midnight in June of 1947, symbolizes how close our planet is to the midnight of nuclear annihilation. In subsequent years it has been moved forward or backward more than a dozen times as the *Bulletin*'s editors have determined that the threat of a major nuclear conflict has increased or decreased. In 1991, with the end of the Cold War between the United States and the Soviet Union, the Clock's hands were moved from ten minutes before midnight back to seventeen minutes before, farther from midnight than it had ever been. In the *Bulletin*'s own history, Mike Moore comments, "By Bulletin standards, that represented an unprecedented burst of enthusiasm and optimism."[15] It appeared as though the threat of nuclear war, the looming danger that had haunted an entire generation, might soon be only an ugly memory.

Now that hope of a nuke-free future is long gone. In February of 2002, the Doomsday Clock moved back to square one — six minutes before twelve, near where it stood in 1947, when the Clock was introduced. We now seem to be closer to Doomsday than we were in 1963, the year after the Cuban Missile Crisis threatened to precipitate a nuclear war between the US and the USSR. In 1963, only the United States and the Soviet Union had a nuclear capability. Today, the list of nations with the ability to deliver the Bomb includes Britain, France, China, India, Pakistan, and Israel. And the roster is growing. It may already include Iran, Libya, and North Korea,[16] often labeled "rogue states."

Iraq's dictator, Saddam Hussein, has for decades been working systematically to acquire nuclear weapons. We have a good idea of what Saddam would like to do with them. On the second day of combat in the Persian Gulf War of 1991, he launched powerful Scud ballistic missiles against Israel, a country that was completely uninvolved in that war. Founded as a haven for those who survived Adolf Hitler's death camps, Israel follows a policy of "never again" — never again will Jews be left defenseless, to be slaughtered at the whim of their neighbors. And the country is so tiny (smaller than all but five of the US's states) that it cannot afford to lose *any* war waged on its territory. It is not surprising, then, that Israel has on three different occasions been ready to respond with its nuclear capability. Whenever their nation's existence is threatened, Israel's leaders are poised to "push the red button." If and when Saddam has the opportunity to lob nuclear weapons into Israel, they will certainly respond in kind.

If we add to the atomic tally sheet the nuclear ambitions of terrorists like Osama bin Laden, the conclusion is difficult to escape. We are perilously approaching the critical mass for a nuclear cataclysm.

In 1965, with the Cold War set into the deep freeze, evangelist Billy Graham wrote, "Modern war is the most highly developed of all sciences. We have perfected our weapons but failed to perfect the men who use them." He continued by posing what was at the time a very pointed question. "There have been men such as Hitler who would have used any means whatsoever to conquer the world. Can we assume that no such man lives now?"[17] No one would even ask this question today. No longer are we tempted to make optimistic assumptions. We *know* that men like Hitler are alive today. In fact, nineteen such men made their presence known on September 11, 2001.

Now imagine the results if an entire city — New York, Washington, D.C., Chicago or Los Angeles — were destroyed by a nuclear explosion. Instead of a few thousand casualties, we might be counting 100,000 dead, with another half-million victims suffering from radiation poisoning. The Doomsday clock now stands at six minutes before twelve. As the United States prepares to weather nuclear attacks not only from rogue states, but also from terrorists like Osama bin Laden, it may be time to move the clock's hands even closer to midnight. The question is no longer "Will someone drop a nuke?" Now it is "*How soon* will the clock strike twelve?" For those who pin their hopes on this world alone, the future may never have looked so grim.

Will some Osama bin Laden or Saddam Hussein fulfill the Bible's visions of the end? Can that be the way God works?

EVIL MEN AND WEAPONS OF MASS DESTRUCTION

Today's terrorism and the rising threat of nuclear conflict may be a foretaste of things to come. Osama bin Laden's dreams of mass annihilation are oddly similar to the Bible's images of future destruction. Perhaps the resemblance is not coincidental. We may be witnessing a dress rehearsal of the script for modern civilization's final act. Many of the judgments recorded in biblical prophecy may be inflicted by nuclear bombs or other weapons of mass destruction. After all, throughout history the Lord has used human agents to fulfill His purposes. And He mixes the miraculous with the mundane. When the biblical hero Joshua took the Amorites by surprise after an all-night march, he used a familiar battlefield tactic to score a decisive victory. But the Lord amplified

Joshua's victory by halting the sun in the middle of the sky so the Amorites could not escape under cover of darkness.[18] The judgments of the last days may form a mosaic of human aggression mixed with direct supernatural intervention.

But would the Lord really use human warmongers to execute His holy judgment? Wouldn't that be like putting the death-row inmates in charge of the prison? Would the Lord really use monsters like Osama bin Laden and Saddam Hussein as His instruments?

He would. Ungodly men can fulfill godly purposes — in spite of themselves. The prophet Habakkuk was horrified to learn that the Lord planned to use the Babylonians as His instruments. He asked, "Why are you silent while the wicked swallow up those more righteous than themselves?"[19] The Lord replied that the Babylonians, in their turn, would be punished. If thousands of years ago God could use the worshippers of a false god to inflict His judgments, He can do so again today. If history is any guide, even some of the most astonishing future judgments may be executed by humans.

Think about it for just a moment. The Bible, a book that claims to be the Word of God, almost two thousand years ago predicted a time of global devastation and the widespread loss of life. One biblical account refers to destruction somehow tied to a mushroom cloud. Another biblical description refers to the basic elements of matter being ignited and consuming much of the earth. What the Bible describes was incomprehensible until a century ago. Now, the war on terrorism has forced us to deal with the proliferation of weapons of mass destruction capable of the devastation predicted throughout the Bible. So how should we respond? In the aftermath of the terrorist attacks many people re-examined their priorities and made the effort to reconcile important relationships. A significant number of people apparently turned to God and the Bible. As the days turned into weeks and the weeks into months, personal security became for many the most pressing concern. How will we ever get life back to "normal" again? Longing for both security and convenience, many people consider technology to be the solution.

Chapter Three Endnotes

[1]Henry Barclay Swete, *The Apocalypse of St. John* (London: Macmillan, 1911), p. 93.

[2]Jonathan Schell, *The Fate of the Earth* (New York: Avon, 1982), p. 49.

[3]2 Peter3:10-13.

[4]Cresson H. Kearney, *Nuclear War Survival Skills*, enlarged and updated (Oak Ridge National Laboratory: U. S. Department of Energy, 1987), ch. 2, pp. 23, 25 (http://www.oism.org/nwss/ s73p913.htm; retrieved June 4, 2002).

[5]Billy Graham, *World Aflame* (Garden City: Doubleday, 1965), pp. 209f.

[6]Peter Wyden, *Day One: Before Hiroshima and After* (New York: Warner Books, 1984), p. 212.

[7]Wyden, *Day One*, p. 212.

[8]Wyden, *Day One*, p. 213.

[9]*Bulletin of the Atomic Scientists* (http://www.bullatomsci.org/

research/qanda/bomsize/html; retrieved November 2001).

[10]Wyden, *Day One*, p. 212. The citation is from the Bhagavad-Gita.

[11]Wyden, *Day One*, p. 216.

[12]Quoted in Paul Kurtz, "Fears of the Apocalypse," Committee for the Scientific Investigation of Claims of the Paranormal (http://www.csicop.org/si/9901/apocalypse.html; retrieved May 28, 2002).

[13]Hamid Mir, "Osama claims he has nukes: If US uses N-arms it will get same response," Dawn: The Internet Edition (http://www.dawn.com/2001/11/10/top1.htm; retrieved May 28, 2002).

[14]afghanradio.com (http://www.afghanradio.com/news/2001/november/nov6ll2001.html; retrieved November 2001).

[15]Mike Moore, "Midnight Never Came: The History of the Doomsday Clock" (http://www.bullatomsci.org/clock/nd95moore1.html; retrieved June 4, 2002).

[16]"Nuclear Weapons: Frequently Asked Questions," Section 7.0, "Nuclear Weapon Nations and Arsenals" http://ohmaster.rau.ac.za/nuclearfaq/Nfaq7.html, retrieved May 28, 2002).

[17]Graham, *World Aflame*, p. 191.

[18]Joshua 10:13b.

[19]Habakkuk 1:13b.

WILL TECHNOLOGY
SAVE US?

In the midst of the war on terrorism, modern technology is monitoring people and their activities as
never before. And it looks as though the high-tech
watchdogs are not going away. The Bible describes
a day when, across the world, even buying a pack of
gum or selling old clothes in a garage sale will be
centrally monitored and controlled.

IF ONLY

Do you remember traveling in the old days . . .
back before 9/11/2001? You went to the airport, the
ticket agent took your luggage, asked some perfunc-
tory questions, glanced at your photo ID, and you
were on your way. Your luggage was thrown onto a
conveyor belt — seldom scanned unless you were
traveling internationally. Your main concern was
whether you would see it at your destination! Your

carry-on luggage was x-rayed by personnel who were well intentioned, but mostly underpaid and poorly trained. When you boarded the airplane, you might have exchanged a casual smile with the pilot as he ran through his pre-flight checklist.

The world of aviation certainly has changed. Today, baggage screeners are employees of the United States government. Airline security personnel examine luggage with bomb detection equipment. Cockpit doors are reinforced. Armed air marshals accompany many flights. Pilots may one day be equipped with firearms. Bottom line — we are going to do whatever it takes to prevent another 9/11.

In the aftermath of the terrorist attacks, we sense a profound regret that we were not prepared. Shouldn't the terrorists have been caught long before they boarded the four planes? Couldn't the CIA have alerted the FBI and immigration officials, in January 2000, that two known terrorists were trying to enter the United States? Khalid Almihdhar and Nawaf Alhazmi came into the country unhindered. Once here, they helped plan the 9/11 attacks and were among the killers who crashed American Airlines Flight 77 into the Pentagon. Shouldn't the FBI have investigated a July 2001 memo from its Phoenix office warning that Arab terrorists might be taking flight lessons in the United States?

A warrant had already been issued for the arrest of Muhammad Atta, who coordinated one of the attacks on the World Trade Center. He was also on the US terrorist watch list, but security personnel at

Logan International Airport were not privy to this information. 9/11 killers Satam Al-Suqami and Waleed Al-Shehri were in the United States illegally. If airport security forces had systematically identified and detained passengers with expired visas or outstanding arrest warrants, the tragedy might have been averted. Had the physical characteristics of these men been captured and automatically compared with the profiles of known terrorists, they might have been apprehended. But at the time, the effort and expense did not seem justified. And many of us were leery of identification systems that might intrude on personal privacy.

Now we have grown all too aware of the existence of well-trained and well-financed operatives determined to destroy the United States and its citizens. Now our safety and security seem more important than nearly anything else. Our thinking has changed, and our society has changed with it.

Before the September 11 atrocity, the American traveling public would not have tolerated the intrusiveness of increased airport security. Imagine being informed, pre-September 11, that you couldn't take a *fingernail file* on an airplane . . . or that you must remove your shoes for inspection prior to entering the terminal . . . or that any passenger might undergo random strip-searching, even an eighty-year-old grandmother or a United States Senator!

The nation's airports provide just one prominent example of our new concern with security and its impact on our daily living. Congress has approved increased financing for the Central Intelligence

Agency and government agencies dedicated to homeland security. Police now possess expanded powers to detain suspected terrorists without pressing criminal charges. Border controls have been tightened. We receive regular warnings of terrorist threats and reminders to keep on the alert. Our need for *identification* and *control* has dramatically altered our everyday living. Now, as never before, we want to know *who people are* long before they might ever attempt to board an airplane and turn it into a missile of death and destruction.

CAN WE REALLY BE SAFE?

As we all know now, the terrorist threat extends well beyond hijacked airplanes. Where will the thugs strike next? Have they smuggled one of Russia's suitcase nukes into our nation? Do they possess the nuclear waste to construct a dirty bomb? Are they capable of raiding one of our nuclear facilities and causing a meltdown? Have they acquired destructive biological and chemical capabilities? Might they contaminate our food supply? How hard would it be for terrorists to transport mad cow disease to America? Where did all the anthrax-laced letters come from, anyway? The questions, like the threats themselves, are endless.

Let's confront the obvious. It is impossible for us to completely protect the infrastructure of our free and open country. After all, it is the same infrastructure that makes our comfortable lifestyles possible. Providing security for the airline industry has been an overwhelming task, and that is just one facet of a multisided labyrinth. The protection of nuclear power plants presents similar challenges. Consider the task of securing our postal system from pipe bombs, or anthrax-laced mail, or . . . you name it.

No foolproof security system exists. When we know *who* people are and can monitor *what* they have been doing, we are at least able to evaluate a potential threat. But identification is not enough to make us secure. People's actions must be tracked and historical profiles (or records of their actions) must be uncovered. Credit card companies already do this by evaluating our financial transactions. They verify our identity, appraise our financial histories, and use that information to determine whether or not to issue us credit cards. If they do, our purchases and payments are then observed on an ongoing basis.

Why not simply expand the database to include more information — and allow government access to this information? In the past, the obstacle has been our concern for personal privacy. But that is changing.

WHATEVER HAPPENED TO PRIVACY?

For years now, technological snooping has grad-ually invaded our lives, and we have gradually grown used to it. When Social Security numbers were first issued in 1934, they faced serious opposi-tion. People regarded them as a potential tool for coercion and control; they noisily protested. Today, our Social Security numbers are requested nearly as often as our names. We readily comply, recalling the nine digits from memory. We can scarcely be part of the US work force without a Social Security number. We must secure a number even for our young children if we want to list them as dependents on our income tax returns. A mortgage or credit card application, a driver's license, life insurance, a bank account — applications for all of these require a Social Security number.

Having long since accepted our ties to Social Security numbers, we are now positioned to grant modern-day technology even more power to intrude. Merchants and creditors scrutinize our purchases. One man told me of a phone call he received at his office. A representative from a major credit card company asked him if he had his card in his possession. When he inquired about their concern, they chronicled for him a long list of purchases made just a few minutes before they placed the call. Naturally, his anxiety surged, but he immediately recognized the names of stores that he and his wife frequented. He expressed his appreciation to the credit card representative, picked up the phone again, and called his wife to ask her what she had bought him that morning!

Since this was an attempt to prevent the fraudulent use of his credit card, he never thought twice about the fact that, moment by moment, the credit card company examined his purchases. What if the United States government had access to the same kind of information? It could track the activities of potential terrorists and intercept them *before* their murderous strikes.

The invasiveness of identification technology has

"hit home" recently with so-called savings cards issued by grocery stores. Just when scanning our purchases became commonplace, grocery stores began to require a personal identification card in order to take advantage of cost-cutting deals. I remember the day a cashier first asked about my "cost-cutter card." As I responded with a questioning stare, I noticed a clerk in the next line scanning a card imprinted with the store logo. The connection between the two became obvious.

The last thing I desire is another card stretching my wallet — or its miniature version decorating my key chain. For some time, I decided to shop at the one local grocer that remained "card-free." This store even tried to attract customers by citing the inconvenience and intrusiveness of the wallet-cluttering cards! They have since issued their own cards.

Such cards seem insignificant, but are they? If we want to buy groceries at a reduced price, we must have the card. But whenever we use the card, we provide businesses and their marketing teams with the opportunity to track every item we purchase. We may not appreciate the erosion of our personal privacy, but we have little energy at the end of the day to do anything about it. The system is having its way, and our day to day purchases are being recorded.

A LESSON FROM GROUND ZERO

On September 16, 2001, Dr. Richard Seelig, a New Jersey surgeon, joined millions of other Americans glued to their televisions, observing the

World Trade Center recovery operations. Fascinated, he watched as workers carefully combed their way through the rubble from the 200,000 tons of twisted and charred steel, 425,000 cubic yards of broken concrete, and 600,000 square feet of shattered and melted window glass that just days earlier had been the Twin Towers of the World Trade Center. If only the rescue and recovery workers could know *where* to dig. If only the injured could signal *where they are*!

As he saw the overwhelming odds against effective recovery operations, Dr. Seelig thought, "There must be a better way. When I heard about the firemen and rescue workers who had written their social-security numbers on their bodies in case they were killed in the rubble, I felt there was a more reliable way to help them get identified."[1]

Dr. Seelig speaks with insight. He serves as a medical consultant for Applied Digital Solutions, a company that manufactures tiny radio-frequency identification chips (RFID's). The chips can be implanted almost anywhere in almost anything — merchandise, money, pets, cattle, human beings — for identification purposes. Toll tags designed for use on highways are an example of RFID's. These high-tech electronic devices operate without a battery. They silently remain in the spot where they have been planted until a scanner, often hand-held, beams the correct radio-wave frequency toward them. Then the tiny amount of energy in the scanner's radio wave activates the individual RFID, prompting it to emit "answering" signals of its own. Depending on the size and power of the unit, a tag can be "read" as far as one hundred feet from the receiver.

What was Dr. Seelig's "more reliable way" of identifying humans? Why not inject RFID chips into them? He promptly tested his idea on himself. He used a syringe to inject two small VeriChip™ RFID's, rice-grain-sized chips manufactured by his company, into his own body. One went into his left forearm, the other into his right leg. He wanted to determine whether his body would accept or reject these high-tech electronic identification tags. His question has been answered . . . the RFID's are still in his body, with no signs of rejection.

A few months later, Jeff and Leslie Jacobs, along with their fourteen-year-old, Derek, proudly became the first family in the world to have VeriChip RFID's injected just under their skin. Nicknamed the Chipsons™, the Florida family has been featured on television's Good Morning America and the Today Show. "We're doing this as a security for us, because we've worked so hard to save my husband's life," said Leslie Jacobs. Her husband, Jeff, has survived a bout with cancer, abdominal operations, a car crash, a degenerative spinal condition, and chronic eye disease. His injuries have forced him to relinquish his dental practice. Leslie Jacobs explains, "We definitely, wholeheartedly believe that this technology will change the world, and it really is an honor to be a pioneer of a technology like this."

Keith Bolton, CEO of Applied Digital Solutions, explains, "In the event that they are in an accident or for some reason unconscious and they can't speak,

then the microchip or VeriChip will speak for them."
Thousands of Americans are already in line, awaiting the implantation of VeriChips, at a cost of $200
per chip.[2]

Jacobs and his family are not concerned that
chips like theirs could be used to invade the privacy
of people's homes or workplaces. Anyone can be
tracked through the Internet and e-mail, credit cards
and cellular phones, they say. Losing a little more
personal privacy is a small price to pay for what one
day may save their lives.[3]

But Applied Digital Solutions, Dr. Seelig's company, doesn't just provide identification tools. It also
assists in locating individuals. The company manufactures the Digital Angel™, which uses Global
Positioning System (GPS) technology to track down
people who may be unconscious or otherwise unable
to communicate. When Washington intern Chandra
Levy suddenly disappeared in May of 2001, she
could have been found promptly, rather than a year
later, claims Dr. Seelig, if she had been wearing a
Digital Angel the size of a small pager. If Wall Street
Journal reporter Daniel Pearl had been equipped
with such a device when he was kidnapped and later
beheaded by Muslim extremists in Pakistan, perhaps
he could have been rescued. Many of the millions of
children reported missing across America might be
located if such a device were commonly used.

In fact, the new devices can save lives — or save
a grade-point average. For parents who need to keep
an eye on their growing children, cellular telephones
will soon incorporate GPS capabilities. Mom or Dad

may readily determine whether Junior is telling the truth when he answers the phone and says he's at the library.

NECESSARY FOR SECURITY?

Since September 11, we have seen that tragedy prompts change. In this case the change goes beyond rapid advances in technology. What we are seeing is a paradigm shift of massive proportions. Our concern used to be privacy, now our primary focus is security...and convenience. We want maximum security without being inconvenienced.

To achieve this goal there has been a myriad of proposals ranging from a national driver's license to an international ID card. As a "stop gap" measure the US Justice Department now photographs and fingerprints people from several countries known to harbor terrorists. It won't be long before such a selective method is considered unfair or even unconstitutional. The solution? Require everyone to have the same form of identification.

The Bible describes a coming time of tragedy — an era of utter devastation throughout the earth, just before Jesus returns. During this time of tribulation, we discover a fascinating prophecy about the coming global economy. People will be required to possess a form of identification tied to a global system. The Bible emphasizes that this system will effectively monitor individual transactions. Why would there be a need for such a system? Could it begin, in part, as a method to combat terrorism as well as other criminal behavior?

If we were able to evaluate what people buy and sell it would give us critical information we need to respond to potential threats worldwide. If Mohammed Atta had gotten the loan he requested to purchase an airplane and a large chemical tank, it would been a big red flag to the authorities.

Before 9/11 we had the technology to track individuals and their purchases. Back then it was not necessary. Personal privacy was the priority. All that has changed. Now we are rapidly heading in a direction that allows for the literal fulfillment of a prophecy the apostle John recorded in the book of Revelation. We will examine that prophecy next.

Chapter Four Endnotes

[1]"Inside Information Concealed in Implants," sundayherald.com (http://www.sundayherald.com/print21807; retrieved June 4, 2002).

[2]Jim Goldman, "Future Family? Florida Family Wants Controversial ID Chip Implants," abcnews.com (http://abcnews.go.com/sections/scitech/TechTV/techtv_verichipfamily020219.html; retrieved June 4, 2002).

[3]"Fla. Family Takes Computer Chip Trip," CBSNEWS.com, May 10, 2002 (http://www.cbsnews.com/stories/2002/05/10/tech/main508641.shtml; retrieved June 4, 2002).

CHAPTER 5

ON YOUR MARK . . .
GET SET . . .

W hen the aged apostle John was exiled to the desolate island of Patmos in the Aegean Sea, he received and recorded the most amazing book found in the entire Bible. Although he was the human author of one of the Gospels, as well as three short letters (*First, Second*, and *Third John*), John is best known for writing the *Revelation*, or *Apocalypse*.

The name Revelation actually means "to remove the veil," or simply "to reveal." Revelation is the unveiling of God's future plans for the world. Its very name indicates it *can* and *ought* to be understood. When a woman wears a veil, it is difficult to distinguish her face clearly until the veil is pulled aside. Likewise, when we study the book of the Revelation the veil is pulled aside; we see the face of the future.

Why is it, then, that many people consider this

final book of the Bible too difficult to understand? I suspect it is the language John uses in his description of what he sees. Imagine what it was like for John, over 1900 years ago, if he was actually *seeing* the day in which we live. When your mode of travel is a donkey or camel, how do you describe a car? When you have never seen an explosion of any kind, how do you explain a nuclear blast? If you see Apache or Blackhawk helicopters in formation, might they not remind you of a swarm of locusts?

SATELLITE AND TELEVISION

John tells us that during the height of the earth's coming seven-year judgment, two prophets will preach in the city of Jerusalem. God will allow them to be overpowered, and they will be put to death. John says that people from all over the world will gaze on their bodies. "The inhabitants of the earth will gloat over them, sending each other gifts . . ."[1] In other words, all over the world people will celebrate the death of God's spokesmen. Was John perhaps a witness to the satellite technology common in our day? How could people all over the world see the same event at the same time without this kind of technology? I thought of this passage when one of the cable news networks captured the brutal beatings of several Palestinians by fellow Arabs. Three men had been accused of providing information to the Israelis. An angry mob beat them to death and then as part of their "victory celebration" they actually displayed the bodies for all to see. The sight of those lifeless bodies half a world away immediately brought John's words to my mind.

A FUTURE REALITY

John's world was totally different from ours, making it difficult to describe what he was actually seeing. He had to call upon his own words and personal experiences in order to define the incredible events he was witnessing. But behind his description of the future, there is a tangible reality. For example, John describes a real-life situation in Revelation 13. He writes that during a time of great distress on the earth two vicious men will dominate the world scene. One of them is known as the Antichrist; the other is called the false prophet. These two will be masters of deception, manipulating people, demanding their allegiance and ultimately their worship. As in the war on terrorism, one of the primary weapons in this struggle will be economic. A time will come when people worldwide will be compelled to possess a form of identification in order to just do their daily shopping. Everyone will be required to have this unique identifier, whether purchasing groceries, filling their gas tanks, or conducting any other financial transaction. We are told that this "mark" will be on either the right hand or the forehead.

This astonishing prophecy has made its way into modern culture through various movies and television, but unfortunately its depiction has rarely been anchored to biblical truth. The Bible ties this mark to the numerical equivalent of the name of a man who will be recognized as the world's leader. The number that represents the name is well known even today — 666.

Such a ruler could have emerged shortly after John wrote these words. He could have used ink that existed in that day and written his number on people's right hands or foreheads. With a world population estimated at that time to be approximately 300 million, it would have been difficult, but not impossible, to force everyone to be part of this system. Rome dominated the world. It is conceivable that compliance could have been forced; the government controlled the marketplaces where people bought and sold their goods.

Even today, a tattoo-based approach for marketplace regulation is available — but with a high-tech twist. Houston lawyer Thomas W. Heeter has been granted US patent no. 5,878,155 for "a method for verifying human identity during electronic sale transactions." Mr. Heeter's idea is simplicity itself. According to this patent, a bar code or a design is tattooed on an individual; and before the sales transaction can be completed, the tattoo is scanned with a scanner.[2]

Mr. Heeter wants to bar code us like a package of Korn Nuts or breath mints. His mark could be put "on any convenient portion of the person's anatomy, preferably the forearm." Most people's first reaction to this idea is, "He's got to be kidding!" Still, Mr. Heeter has gotten his patent. Why? He is able to point out that his idea is actually practical. In an era of e-money and identity theft, criminals can easily steal not only our money, but also our line of credit, purloining money we don't even have. He's not the only inventor searching for a foolproof identification system.

The Bible tells us the day will come when people must bear a mark in order to buy or sell. Whether the mark turns out to be a complex computer chip or a simple tattoo, we can already see that day coming.

BIOMETRICS: I KNOW YOU!

What will it take for us to feel secure once again? The fact is, we may never again be able to take our security for granted. Tom Ridge, director of the US Office of Homeland Security, has said it definitively — the threat of terrorism will not end in the foreseeable future.

How, then, might we protect ourselves against counterfeits who creep into our midst with the sole purpose of destroying us? How might we foil their plans to present a false identity? ID cards have the capacity to store a wealth of information, as well as potential for connection to an online database, but they inevitably will be stolen or forged. Even RFID's or other high-tech chips implanted under people's skin could be counterfeited. That's why *biometrics* seems to be the wave of the future.

Biometrics identifies people by recording their unique physical characteristics. Dozens of distinctive traits make each of us different from other human beings. For example:

- fingerprints
- handwriting
- hand shape
- facial appearance
- voice patterns
- DNA patterns
- the shape of our ear canals
- the shape, arrangement, and condition of our teeth
- the pattern of blood vessels visible on the retina at the back of our eyes
- the pattern of lines on the irises that give us our eye color
- our unique body scent that devices can detect and perfume can't mask

The list continues. Biometric identification has existed for well over a hundred years. Even prior to precision fingerprinting, prison officials painstakingly recorded anatomical measurements to aid in identifying criminals. But the computer age has transformed biometrics. Distinguishing identity from fingerprints or other biometric data formerly required careful study by human experts. It could take weeks to generate results. Now computers recognize people in less than a second. If you don't like your children using your computer, you can buy the Siemens ID Mouse, a computer mouse that reads fingerprints. It won't let unauthorized users log on.

An ID badge, card, or chips are items we possess, or *have*. They can easily be stolen. A personal identification number (PIN) or other ID number is something we memorize or *know*. If we can remember it, a criminal can probably crack it. But biometrics relies on who we *are*. Thus, its use has become increasingly prevalent when security and convenience are essential.

London's Heathrow Airport has tested iris-recognition technology with about 2,000 passengers who routinely fly to and from North America. The image of a person's iris remains in a computer, and a camera verifies the person's eye against that image. The EyeTicket Corporation, located in McLean, Virginia, markets similar technology for airport access, as well as for ticketless admission to sports and entertainment venues. Face-recognition systems developed by such companies as Visionics and Graphco operate in several airports across our nation.

This type of technology first came to public notice during Superbowl 2001 at the Raymond James Stadium in Tampa, Florida. Cameras positioned around the stadium automatically digitized the faces of over 100,000 fans and compared the images with criminal mug shots and photos of known offenders. The general public reacted, calling the surveillance a "computerized police lineup." Then, in June of 2001, 36 cameras were mounted on 7th Street in Tampa's Ybor City area in order to compare facial characteristics of people on the street with known offenders. Several national monument locations utilize similar cameras as a safeguard against terrorism. The United States war on terrorism has diminished the initial opposition to such surveillance.

This is just the beginning. The possibilities are endless; any number of our distinctive personal characteristics, from the shape of our ears to the genetic patterns in our DNA, can be used to identify us accurately. But the next step goes well beyond identification. It includes the ability to *locate* individuals, as well.

ARE IDENTIFICATION AND HISTORY ENOUGH?

Remember the Jacobs family, discussed in the previous chapter? Now that they have their VeriChip implants, medical personnel can quickly pull up their medical records, even if they are found unconscious and without any identification documents. The RFID's implanted just under their skin will be their ID documentation. With biometric identification, a camera's glance at a terrorist's fingerprint or facial appearance or hand shape could instantly transport his records from a government computer.

But what if that terrorist has kept his nose clean? What if he hasn't overstayed his visa? What if he's never gotten into trouble with the law? What if he was selected for a terrorist operation specifically because his superiors know the database *doesn't* have any negative information about him? To recognize a person like that as a terrorist, we would have to be able to tell what he's doing *right now*. For example, we would need to know what he is doing with his money. That would be essential. Terrorism is a very expensive business.

MAXIMUM SECURITY

To know what is going on inside a secret criminal enterprise, we must follow its money trail. Rather than "show me the money," it's "show me where the money is going!" For this reason the United States government requires banks to report cash deposits of $10,000 or more. And when someone pays cash for an airline ticket, that purchase is flagged, the question being "Does this individual have a reason to avoid leaving a financial trail?"

Financial transactions are easily traced. In fact, detailed tracking of fiscal dealings is already common. In the future, this tracking could be fine-tuned to become a powerful weapon of control. A recent incident involving a suspicious purchase illustrates the advantages of such monitoring.

Shortly before Halloween in 2001, an Arab immigrant purchased $15,000 worth of candy at Costco stores in Wayne and Hackensack, New Jersey. Costco employees were suspicious of such a large purchase at Halloween. They wondered whether the man might lace the candy with poison or anthrax, then distribute it to children or return it to the stores to be sold to unsuspecting shoppers. They reported the sale to local police, who reported it to the FBI. Both the man and the candy were later found. The man was detained on immigration charges.[3]

The key here is that this man's purchases appeared suspicious *by themselves*. The observant Costco employees had no way of knowing what he might or might not be buying elsewhere. If he had taken the time to buy $15 worth of candy at 1,000 stores, no one would have become suspicious.

Similarly, many terrorist activities do not appear suspicious unless they are viewed in combination with other acts. A man buys a large quantity of fertilizer. Not a particularly suspect transaction. A different man buys a lot of fuel oil. That, too, might be ordinary. But knowledge that the man stocking up on fertilizer lives in an apartment, and that the man buying the fuel oil is his roommate, would immediately shed a clearer light on their intentions. No one act is especially sinister, but in combination they merit further investigation.

And only someone with general access to commercial transactions could catch that combination. Better yet, a well-designed computer program, tracing everyone's purchases, could flag a suspicious-looking pattern of acquisitions. If *all* purchases were electronically processed and linked to biometric identification, then it would be possible to trace every purchase and link it with every other purchase by that person, or by his associates. Life could become tough for terrorists!

What I have just described is not as futuristic or as far-fetched as it might seem. There are credible reports that Project Echelon, operating since 1971, routinely intercepts massive amounts of information every day. Operating under the direction of intelligence agencies from several countries, including the United States and Britain, this secret network indiscriminately gathers information from billions of e-mail messages, faxes, satellite transmissions, telephone calls and internet downloads, and then quickly processes the data, searching for keywords.[4] Imagine this same approach being taken with financial transactions. The kind of sophisticated terrorist tracking we have discussed above could soon become routine.

FROM IDENTIFICATION TO LOCATION

If the day comes when biometric IDs and computer databases are combined with global positioning (GPS) technology, anti-terrorist officials will have a new high-tech tool with powers beyond Dick Tracy's wildest dreams. Not only will they know who people are and what they have done. They will also know *where people are right now*, and what they are doing. The widely used GPS system can pinpoint the location of a car, cell phone, or anything else that carries a GPS module. The Federal Communications Commission has already begun mandating GPS modules in cellular telephones.[5] Soon, implanted GPS devices could allow authorities to determine an individual's exact location.

Imagine what might happen when a security analyst in Washington, D.C. notices a warning on her computer, alerting her that three men on her watch list have arrived at the same Boston airport in three separate taxis. These men know each other and are all suspected of association with the same terrorist group. Quickly pulling up a real-time record of their movements and financial transactions, she notices that they have all bought tickets on the same plane.

Then they all take seats in the same waiting area. They are close enough to see each other, but never approach each other. They seem to be treating each other as strangers.

Wondering whether this could be a coincidence, she begins to enter a quick database query describing the scenario. Within seconds, the computer could tell her that this pattern of behavior has previously been found *only* in cases of attempted terrorist hijackings. But she doesn't get to complete her query. While she is still typing it in, the computer issues another automatic alert, flashing red at the top of her screen: "Suspected hijacking in progress: ticket-holders Muhammad al-Jazeera, Isamail Nazeem, Hadrami Hamsar. Detain immediately for questioning."

Right away, the security analyst grabs the phone for a quick call to notify the airport police in Boston. She's just double-checking, of course. The airport police have already received the same alert. They know which men to pick up, and they know where they're sitting.

In a time when terrorists are well trained, using advanced technology in their quest to destroy us, the urge is strong to strike back with every available high-tech tool. Will concerns over loss of privacy hold back the use of biometric IDs, centralized databases, and GPS devices? In the face of the ongoing terrorist threat, that seems very doubtful.

HOW CONVENIENT

Security has trumped privacy as a result of the

war on terrorism. But security is also getting a tremendous assist from a growing movement to make life simpler. We want security and we want convenience.

In College Station, Texas, several grocery stores are pioneering the ultimate in easy shopping. People who shop in these grocery stores don't need cash or a credit card. They get a cart, select their groceries and then they leave without ever going through a long checkout line. Sounds like a free shopping spree, doesn't it? Check again.

Remember the RFIDs or radio frequency IDs we discussed in the last chapter? Here is how it works. A person who uses this service registers a credit card that uses a finger scan as identification. When he is finished shopping his finger is scanned, activating a radio frequency transmitter that records his purchases. It then computes the total without even taking the items out of his cart! Each food item has its own unique RFID which is "read" by the transmitter, and the total is then charged to the credit card.

WHAT WILL THE MARK MEAN?

Can we be certain that modern technology will be used to promote the mark - 666? The answer in a word, is - no. We cannot be certain. The buying and selling of goods might eventually be controlled and monitored in a way unimaginable to us today. But our hi-tech world offers several options for the fulfillment of John's prophecy even with a world population of over six billion people. For reasons that are easy to understand, the world appears more willing than ever before to accept the intrusive technology that such a system employs.

The coming ID system the Bible describes will not be voluntary. It will be a visible pledge of allegiance to a world system under the control of the man who establishes his credentials by brokering a peace agreement in the Middle East. It is difficult to envision someone with this kind of power and influence. We cannot fathom this happening until we understand what the Bible says about this man. As we will see in the next chapter, he will be a leader like the world has never, ever seen.

Chapter Five Endnotes

[1]Revelation 11:9-10.

[2]"Method for verifying human identity during electronic sale transactions," USPTO Patent Full-Text and Image Database (http://patft.uspto.gov/netacgi/nph-Parser?Sect1= PTO2&Sect2=HITOFF&p=1&u=/netahtml/search- bool.html&r=4&f=G&l=50&col=AND&d=ft00&s1=Heeter&s2=Th omas&OS=Heeter+AND+Thomas&RS=Heeter+AND+Thomas; retrieved May 23, 2002).

[3]The AFU and Urban Legends Archive (http://www.urbanlegends. com/ulz/candy.html; retrieved May 23, 2002).

[4]"Answers to Frequently Asked Questions (FAQ) about Echelon," echelonwatch (http://www.aclu.org/echelonwatch/faq.html; retrieved May 29, 2002).

[5]"SyChip Claims Smallest Full-Function GPS Module," ebnonline. com (http://www.ebnonline.com/ecomponents/semiconews/story/ OEG20001106S0028; retrieved June 4, 2002).

CHAPTER 6

LOOKING
FOR A LEADER

The Scriptures give us an unforgettable portrait of a uniquely gifted leader who will in the days to come negotiate a peace treaty between Israel and her neighbors. This man will achieve something that seems impossible. He will craft an agreement that will satisfy *everyone*. With tension spreading across the globe, more and more people are looking for just such a leader.

IN THE MIDST OF TRAGEDY

Before the September 11 terrorist attacks, some regarded George W. Bush as a President unable to command the respect of the American public. In the days following the attacks, Mr. Bush handled the crisis with natural and commanding agility. His approval rating from the American public rose above ninety percent. That surpasses the popularity of any other President since the beginning of poll taking!

Other leaders also quickly took center stage when the World Trade Center became a pile of rubble. New York Mayor Rudy Giuliani anchored ground zero with decisive and compassionate fervor. New Yorkers immediately forgot the unpleasant tabloid stories about their mayor's personal life. They looked to him to restore the soul of their city. Giuliani did that. He did it so well, in fact, that many New Yorkers were ready to revise the mayoral term limits to let Giuliani serve an additional term.

Today, the entire planet is looking for effective leaders like these. Our world is in turmoil. We have grown weary of the constant tension spawned by radical Islamic fundamentalism. We have been horrified by the escalating Israeli-Palestinian conflict. The person who can untie this tangled knot will be everyone's hero.

The world desperately longs for a leader who can bring peace to the Middle East. In fact, the world yearns for a leader who can bring peace between India and Pakistan . . . Russia and Chechnya . . . Roman Catholics and Protestants in Northern Ireland . . . and who can defuse other flashpoints. People crave a leader who can bring peace to the entire planet. Such a commander would not only capture the hearts and minds of his fellow countrymen, but he would capture hearts and minds around the world.

The world waits.

The Bible tells us that just such a leader *will* emerge on the world scene, coming to the forefront in a time much like today. A charismatic personality, a gifted communicator, a masterful diplomat, this leader will enjoy the endorsement of the religious establishment, as well as powerful political allies. He will assume power as the leader of a ten-nation European federation that recreates the ancient Roman Empire. He will rapidly seize power over three European nations, with an additional seven countries supporting him.

The Bible also tells us that this man will rise to leadership following the miraculous disappearance of all true believers in Jesus Christ from the earth. Evil and deception will flourish as never before.

This man will not be like any other leader in history. First of all, this dictator will be personally directed by the devil. He will be energized, controlled, and dominated by Satan. But despite his uniqueness, he will exhibit many of the same leadership qualities that have made other men powerful.

What is this man's name? We don't know. What we do know is his defined purpose. His ultimate goal is to oppose Jesus Christ; that is why this leader is called the Antichrist.

In order to comprehend the depths of the deception that will energize the Antichrist, consider Osama bin Laden and his ardent followers. Bin Laden has convinced thousands of young men to pursue jihad, or holy war, against the West. In the name of Allah, bin Laden orchestrated the terrorist attacks of September 11, 2001. Using his interpretation of the Koran and other Islamic writings, he convinced Muhammad Atta and eighteen other young men to come to America on a terrorist mission. They spent several years waiting patiently and planning meticulously before executing their homicidal hijackings. These men were brainwashed! They were convinced they were doing the work of Allah. They sincerely believed that upon completion of their mission they would immediately enter heaven as martyrs.

Mesmerized by the lies of bin Laden, these men murdered thousands of innocent people. When the news of the hijackings reached the world, other radical Muslim fundamentalists celebrated, dancing and rejoicing at this "judgment by Allah." Such behavior might seem unthinkable, but it is another example of the demonic deception that an effective leader can disseminate. But the Antichrist will be far better at controlling and manipulating people's minds than even Osama bin Laden.

THE NUMBER OF THE NAME

Through the centuries, Bible students have attempted to find out who the Antichrist will be, searching for the identity of this fascinating figure. Their interest is understandable. After all, he will be a pivotal figure in the fulfillment of biblical prophecy. As we have noted, the Bible does not tell us his name. It says that the letters of his name, in their numerical value, will add up to the total 666. But that does not enable us to discover his actual name. Irenaeus, who was closely connected to the biblical Apostle John, wisely stated:

So it is more certain, and less hazardous, to wait for the fulfillment of the prophecy, rather than to make guesses, and hunt around for any names that may pop up. After all, *many* names can be found that add up to the number mentioned, and the question will still remain unsolved. If we find many names that correspond to the number, the question remains: which of them is the name of the coming man?[1]

History is full of guesses about this future ruler's name — so many of them that they underscore Irenaeus' point. But the Bible seems to indicate that the number 666 is to be used for verification. In other words, people who have *already* recognized the Antichrist and know his name can use the number 666 to confirm their conclusion. They will be able to validate their judgment by adding up the numerical values of the letters of his name. So how will people recognize the Antichrist to begin with, if not by juggling letters and numbers? The Bible answers the question by providing a detailed description of his life and career.

A TIME OF CRISIS

First of all, the Bible tells us that this coming leader will appear suddenly during a period of incredible stress. The tension that Americans felt immediately following the 9/11 attacks might begin to parallel the trauma of daily life in this yet future time. As mentioned earlier, all true believers will have been taken to heaven, removing from the earth their positive influence. A seemingly endless sequence of disasters will bombard every corner of the world. *Every one* of these crises will be as horrific as the 9/11 attacks — or even worse. Again and again, men and women will wake to a morning newscast that reports more catastrophes. Often, those disasters will have destroyed a large percentage of the earth's population.

Although energized by evil, angelic powers, the Antichrist will also show the same management traits that have marked influential rulers in every period of world crisis. Columnists and editorial writers will doubtless compare his methods to those of men such as Mayor Giuliani, President Bush, and England's Prime Minister Tony Blair. Historians will compare him to the great wartime leaders of earlier generations, like President Franklin D. Roosevelt and Great Britain's Winston Churchill. On the debit side of the sheet, he will also resemble dictators Adolf Hitler, Joseph Stalin, and China's Chairman Mao — and the list could easily continue. Above all, this man will *rule*. The Bible calls him "the ruler who will come." He will seem to the world to be the greatest ruler in all history. This man will know how to *lead*.

MARKS OF AN EFFECTIVE LEADER

Leadership is a mystical quality, a combination of personal skills, innate magnetism and a heavy dose of circumstance. In this time of need and grief, the New York mayor — through personal presence, an overflowing heart and just the right words — has stepped forward to lead his city from despair to determination.[2]

With these words, commentator Marc Fisher pinpoints three key characteristics of the person able to lead in time of crisis. First, such a leader must be must be a good *communicator*, able to persuade the people to follow his lead. Second, he must show *concern*. People must sense that he identifies with them and feels what they feel. Third, and perhaps most importantly, he must be *charismatic*. He must possess a personal magnetism that draws people to him, compelling them to trust him.

Communicator

When disaster strikes, people immediately search for someone who can express their feelings and confront their fears. If such a leader appears, men and women are ready to listen to him, regardless of any doubts they may have had about him in the past. Grasping for the confidence and hope they sense in their leader, people believe that he can "fix it" for them. Warren Bennis, Director of the University of Southern California's Leadership Institute, says:

Leaders deal in hope. Hope means to lead people to invest in the future; and that is what makes winning ball clubs, winning countries and winning organizations. When things are bad, it is not the job of leaders to be gloomy and pessimistic . . . you have to do the best you can to give direction with meaning.[3]

President Ronald Reagan, elected to the presidency at a moment when America was under attack by Muslim extremists, knew how to deal in hope. When fundamentalist Muslims seized the US embassy in Iran and kidnapped its personnel, the response of the previous President, Jimmy Carter, seemed hesitant and wavering. In contrast, Mr. Reagan's decisiveness made people feel secure, empowered. Because he knew how to display a forthright, confident, and optimistic face to an often-hostile world, Reagan became one of America's best-loved Presidents.

In the aftermath of September 11, New York Mayor Rudolf Giuliani demonstrated the same ability to communicate hope. A harsh critic of America's reaction to 9/11 nonetheless praised Mayor Giuliani's response:

Within hours of the attacks in New York, he was out on the streets, surveying the damage and encouraging rescuers. He never hesitated or made his personal well being a top priority. That was real leadership. And, in the days after the tragedy, Giuliani has continued to shine. He says

the right things, is specific and leaves off
the sugar-coating.[4]

Traits like these made Mayor Giuliani *Time* mag-
azine's legendary "Man of the Year." Like Mayor
Giuliani, Prime Minister Tony Blair, and other leaders who have risen to new prominence in the wake of
September 11, the Antichrist will be a talented communicator. He will arrive on the scene promising
peace. And he will deliver peace. He will broker a
treaty promising much-needed stability to the powder keg of the Middle East.

One day, maybe in the not too distant future, people will be glued to their televisions to hear an
address from the man who will have done what no
one else has been able to do. He will be the "father"
of a peace agreement between Israel and her Arab
neighbors. We can almost anticipate what the news
headlines will say. "Finally! Peace in the Middle
East!" Or, "Israel's Security Guaranteed." Another
news alert headline might read, "Agreement to Share
the Temple Mount Completes the Peace Agreement."

With Israel at the epicenter of international concern, we can almost sense that headlines like these
may not be that far off. Can you imagine what this
consummate politician will say at the news confer-
ence to announce the final details of the agreement?
With a smile on his face, he will command the attention of the world community; his words will certainly
fall on receptive ears. "Ladies and gentlemen, the
nations of the world long for peace, and today we
have peace in the Middle East. The nation of Israel

has agreed to remove the walls that have divided Israel and Palestine. In exchange, the Palestinians will allow Christians to build a church and Israel to build a temple on Haram al-Sharif or the Temple Mount."

A message of hope like this presented by a gifted communicator would have a profound and far-reaching impact on the entire civilized world. He would become an instant hero and a leader that people would naturally trust.

But the Bible tells us he will soon make a mockery of his promises of peace. Under this man's leadership, people will enjoy apparent peace and safety — for a while. Then, the Bible tells us, destruction will come upon them suddenly. By the time this travesty becomes clear, the world will have been brainwashed by this leader's magnificent words and what appears to be genuine concern for everyone.

Concerned

To lead effectively in troubled times, a leader must also show empathy for his people. He must demonstrate that he really cares. The people must see that he shares their worries and grief. During the Civil War, President Lincoln once wept when he learned that three hundred Confederate soldiers had died in battle. The man who had brought him the message could not understand why he would weep over the death of his *enemies*. Lincoln replied, "Sir, you have a very small heart." Lincoln showed that he had a big heart. That is why, over one hundred years later, he is still one of America's best-loved

Presidents. Similarly, the soaring popularity of George W. Bush stems, in part, from the compassion he shows.

When the future world leader enters the political fray in the Middle East he will have the capacity to endear himself to Jews and Arabs alike. The Palestinians will feel they have someone who understands their frustration and sense of despair. Many Israelis will look at this man as the embodiment of the promised Messiah. People, entire nations, will trust this man and his leadership.

Beyond the veneer this world leader will *not* have a big heart. His heart will be full of self-love, to the point where he will eventually claim to be God. But, like many politicians before him, the Antichrist will have an extraordinary ability to deceive people. No doubt he will find it easy to summon up a moving tribute or eulogy, delivered in a voice cracking with emotion, when it suits his purpose. To the adoring crowds, this master of deception may indeed seem like another Lincoln.

Charismatic

Charisma. It may be complicated to define, but it is not difficult to recognize. It's the personal magic that arouses special loyalty and enthusiasm for a leader. President John F. Kennedy had charisma. Ronald Reagan had so much charisma that he was dubbed the "Teflon President." Criticism just wouldn't stick to him! Possibly no American President had more charisma than Franklin D.

Roosevelt, who was sent to the White House for four consecutive terms as he led the country through the Great Depression and World War II. On the other hand, Presidents Herbert Hoover and Richard Nixon registered somewhere below zero on the charisma scale and suffered political meltdown.

On the international scene, British Prime Minister Tony Blair has charisma. Since September 2001, he has led with "the charisma to pull off things that may seem impossible at first," in the words of one commentator.[5] He has been so decisive and energetic in building support for the war on terrorism that he has broken popularity records in his own country. And in America, where European politicians are usually ignored, an opinion poll showed that half of all Americans would vote for Mr. Blair if he were to run for the office of President of the United States![6]

But in the coming world crisis, the Middle East power broker will leave Blair's vaunted charisma in the dust. In his vision of future events, the apostle John saw how this man will fill people with astonishment and admiration. John's description cuts through the veneer and recognizes this man to be, in reality, a wild animal or a "beast." "The entire earth was astonished and followed the beast . . . and they also worshipped the beast and said, 'Who is like the beast? Who can make war against him?'"[7] Abraham Lincoln remarked, "You can fool some of the people all the time, and all of the people some of the time, but you cannot fool all of the people all the time." This man will nearly succeed in proving Lincoln wrong! People will feel themselves irresistibly drawn to his presence and power.

The Antichrist will be so personally impressive that the Bible uses superhuman imagery to describe him. The book of Revelation compares him to a leopard, bear, and lion rolled into one! In portraits like this, we catch a vivid glimpse of a person with all the aggressive energy of a hungry wild animal. In the space of just two-and-a-half years, this man will accomplish more than most politicians will achieve in a lifetime. His resumé will include the resolution of the Mideast conflict and the implementation of a strategy for developing a global government. Under his leadership, the world will one day be politically unified and all nations will be as one.

IN THE FACE OF DANGER

At moments of intense crisis, good leaders seem fearless, even cocky, when their own lives are at stake. While campaigning for the presidency in 1912, Theodore Roosevelt was shot at close range by John Schrank, a New York saloonkeeper. Roosevelt insisted on finishing his speech — *then* he went to the hospital, where he had to remain for eight days.

Years later, in 1933, bricklayer Guiseppe Zangara fired five shots at Theodore's cousin, Franklin D. Roosevelt, who had just been elected President. Zangara's shots missed Roosevelt, but mortally wounded Chicago Mayor Anton Cermak, who was standing nearby. Roosevelt, who was crippled by polio and confined to a wheelchair, could not dodge Zangara's bullets, but he never flinched. He stared straight into the eyes of his would-be assassin. Then he turned to comfort Mayor Cermak, embracing him as the mayor was taken to the hospital.

When John Hinkley shot the then recently inaugurated President, Ronald Reagan, in 1981, Mr. Reagan's life was in serious danger. But he light-heartedly reassured his family and the nation. "I hope you guys are Republicans," he remarked to his doctors as he was atop a gurney on his way to surgery to remove Hinckley's bullet from his chest. Later, he joked with his wife, Nancy, saying, "Honey, I forgot to duck."

Similarly, in the days following the terrorist attack on the Twin Towers, New York Mayor Giuliani earned the loyalty of his city and the admiration of his nation by refusing to worry about his own safety. As one prominent New Yorker put it, "Rudolph Giuliani is the personification of courage."[8]

Leaders like these are giants in the eyes of their nations because they confront personal danger without fear. Similarly, this demonically energized leader will laugh in the face of disaster and death. He will personally march his troops into battle across the globe, something common in earlier centuries but unheard of among today's heads of state. And this man will not lead from the rear; he will enthusiastically expose himself to the dangers of the battlefield. His final military opponent will be Jesus Himself. But that will still not detour him from his goal — to win at all costs. He'll never reach that goal. Not when he's fighting against Jesus Christ!

The Bible tells us he will be captured, tried, and condemned.

BACK FROM THE GRAVE

This false messiah's ability to laugh at death will provide a dimension no other leader's bravado can match. He will be the first world leader to be able to claim that he has conquered death itself. When he appears on the scene this man will receive what appears to be a fatal wound — but he will be healed. Talk about a political resurrection! From the outset, people will regard him as utterly amazing. They will want to follow him wherever he leads. He will have a special charisma beyond that of any other earthly leader.

Never having seen a politician return from the dead, we can only imagine how deeply his followers will be impressed by his fatal wound, still visible, but "healed." But men such as Iraq's Uday Hussein may provide us with a clue. Uday is scarcely a household word in America, but in Iraq he's big political news. Yet just a few years ago, he was politically dead — and barely escaped physical death. The son of Iraqi dictator Saddam Hussein, Uday used to be notorious as a playboy, a man who devoted his life to gambling and womanizing. His greatest victories were scored in the Iraqi black market. Even in Iraq, he was not well regarded.

Then, in December 1996, Uday was gunned down and left for dead in a Baghdad suburb. Several of his bodyguards were killed in the attack, and

Uday was not expected to survive. When it became clear that he would live after all, doctors said he would never walk again. After several surgeries, Uday has re-emerged in reasonable health. And his unlikely survival has created a wave of public sympathy and enthusiasm. Along with a new life, Uday has crafted a new, more serious image and a political career for himself. As a result, the despised playboy has become a respected national leader. Today Uday is a wildly popular member of the Iraqi National Assembly and a prime candidate to succeed his father as leader of the world's number-two oil power.[9]

The coming false messiah will enjoy the applause that comes from cheating death. But his glory will be all the greater than Uday Hussein's, because he will seem to have actually come back from the grave!

As the months have passed since 9/11, the political landscape has dramatically changed. Nations have taken their stand for or against the war on terrorism. The battle is far from over, and future efforts will be increasingly more dangerous. With tensions rising across the globe, the stage may already be set for the entrance of the Antichrist. Once he brokers a peace agreement between Israel and her neighbors, his political prowess will be unsurpassed.

Where will this much-anticipated leader's grand entrance take place? Where will he come from? We will find the answer to these questions in the next chapter.

Chapter Six Endnotes

[1] Irenaeus, *Against Heresies*, 5, 30, 3.

[2] Marc Fisher, "From New York, a Stirring Lesson in Leadership," *The Washington Post*, September 22, 2001 (http://www.washingtonpost.com/ac2/wp-dyn?pagename=article&node=&contentId=A7201-2001Sep21; retrieved June 4, 2002).

[3] "Bennis: 'Leaders Deal in Hope' — Acclaimed Expert Addresses Benefit on Safeguarding Employees Post-9/11" (http://www.marshall.usc.edu/Web/Press.cfm?doc_id=4025; retrieved June 4, 2002).

[4] Tom Gutting, "Bush Has Failed to Lead USA," *Texas City Sun*, Sept. 22, 2001.

[5] "Person of the Year: Tony Blair," geocities.com (http://www.geocities.com/rmcoker/reviewperson.html; retrieved June 4, 2002).

[6] "Tony Blair and the Churchill Factor," Linguapress (http://members.aol.com/linguapress/Blairfactor.htm; retrieved June 4, 2002).

[7] Revelation 13:3f.

[8] David Letterman, "One Word: Courage" (excerpts from David Letterman's monologue upon returning to the air, Monday Sept. 17, 2001), *LawTechnologyNews* (http://www.lawtechnews.com/october01/tech_support_p16b.html; retrieved June 4, 2002).

[9] Sue Masterman and Bassam Barhoum, "Back from the Grave," ABC Online News (http://abcnews.go.com/sections/world/ Daily News/uday000328.html; retrieved June 4, 2002).

CHAPTER 7

THE EUROPEAN UNION AND THE UNITED STATES IN PROPHECY

If you think having a family reunion is difficult when you have been scattered all over the world for nearly 2000 years, try getting the people in various neighborhoods to agree to form one big neighborhood. The Jews were scattered all over the world, but in 1948 they had a family reunion. The unification of countries throughout Europe over the past decade is no less miraculous.

Imagine for a moment a typical neighborhood, where people cherish their privacy and have their own unique culture. Your task is to unite these diverse groups under one umbrella.

Let me complicate the task a bit more. Each neighborhood has its own language and its own unique currency, and there have been security fences between these neighborhoods for decades, even hundreds of years. There has also been a history of bad blood between many of the families in these various neighborhoods.

To begin, you must get the people in these neighborhoods to agree to be part of this larger group. When these people and their families "sign on" they agree . . . to remove their fences, have a single homeowners' association, and accept a governing body that will oversee all the neighborhoods together. In addition, each neighborhood also agrees to have their residents turn in their own unique money for a new currency, which will be used in all of the neighborhoods! Sounds impossible, doesn't it?

During the past ten years, something much like this has happened in Europe. It's called the European Union, established in 1993. Before then, of course, each country in Europe had its own unique history and culture. Its own language. Its own government. Its own currency, sometimes going back hundreds of years.

But now they have come together.

Can you imagine giving up dollars and cents for newly invented money, shared with other countries? Giving up your country's independence, letting other nations have a vote on issues that affect your life and your pocketbook? Can you think what it would be like to vote for local representatives who would then meet in some other country where their influence could be drowned by votes from other countries? Can you imagine risking your life to fight in an army designed mostly to protect *other* nations, not your own? All this is happening in Europe today.

After many hundreds of years, the world's greatest empire appears to be returning. It's called the Roman Empire. In its original heyday, this empire was so vast and powerful that the Mediterranean Sea was jokingly called a Roman lake. The Roman Peace, enforced by a powerful army, kept clans and communities across Asia, Europe, and Africa secure under a single central government. Now the European Union may be on a path that will make all this happen again.

This revival of the Roman Empire is amazing in itself. But it's also an astonishing fulfillment of biblical prophecy. The Bible predicts that the Roman Empire will be instrumental in bringing a Middle East peace agreement. Today, the European Union (EU) already offers a smaller, but modern-day version of the Roman Empire. And the EU has been a major force working for peace in the Middle East — especially since 9/11/2001! In the prophetic book of Daniel, the Bible gives us a detailed picture of the role this ancient empire will play *in the future*.

THE FUTURE IN A DREAM

Throughout the history of the Bible, God often spoke to men and women through dreams. For example, when King Herod planned to kill Jesus as a young child, God warned Joseph in a dream to escape to Egypt with Jesus and Mary. God also sent visions, "waking dreams," to guide His followers. Most of the last book of the Bible, the book of the Revelation, records a vision of the end times that

Jesus Christ gave to the apostle John. Of course, today there are people who claim that they have received new revelations from God in dreams and visions. Typically, their predictions do not come true and their teachings may well contradict what the Bible says, revealing these are actually false prophets.

Centuries before Jesus Christ was born, God communicated in a dream to the great Babylonian King Nebuchadnezzar. It described the world empires that would rise and fall until Jesus Christ comes and rules the earth. The Lord showed Nebuchadnezzar a huge statue with a head of gold, chest and arms of silver, belly and thighs of bronze, legs of iron, and feet of iron mixed with clay. Then a rock struck the statue's feet, smashing them, and the entire statue broke up and was pulverized. The wind blew away its fragments without leaving a trace. But the rock that struck the statue became a huge mountain and filled the entire earth.

King Nebuchadnezzar was an idol-worshipper— he was not qualified to understand this symbolic message from God. But God revealed the dream's meaning to the prophet Daniel, who in turn told the king. The different sections of the colossus represented four great empires, Daniel said. Four huge territories, each ruled by a single person. Daniel told Nebuchadnezzar what each of these successive empires would be like. The first was the Babylonian Empire of Nebuchadnezzar himself, who ruled for forty-three years, beginning about six hundred years before Christ was born. "You are that head of gold,"

Daniel told King Nebuchadnezzar.[1]

That head of gold still influences us today. The Babylonians were scientific and mathematical innovators who based many of their measurements on the number sixty. It is because of them that we have sixty minutes in each hour and sixty seconds in each minute.

Three more empires were to follow Nebuchadnezzar's Babylonian Empire. Each of them swallowed up and expanded the territory of the empire before it. The second empire was the Persian Empire of Cyrus, centered in modern-day Iran. Cyrus conquered Babylon in 539 BC. Like the Babylonian Empire, the Persian Empire has had a lasting impact. Its official language, Aramaic, spread from Egypt to India and later became Jesus' native tongue. Part of the Old Testament is written in Aramaic, and a number of Aramaic words are found in the New Testament.

Then came the Greek empire of Alexander the Great, who defeated the Persians and took over their empire in 331 BC. This empire spread Greek art, culture, and language throughout the Mediterranean world, so that when the New Testament came to be written, it was written in Greek. The various writers of the New Testament used common Greek in order to reach the largest possible number of people.

Finally, the Roman Empire, under Caesar Augustus, completed its absorption of the Greek empire by 31 BC, about three decades before the birth of Jesus. The influence of the Roman Empire is still obvious today. Our English alphabet is borrowed from the Romans. And about half the words in English come from Latin, the Romans' language. The Roman Empire has never been followed by another world empire — just as Nebuchadnezzar's dream predicted.

What about the rock that destroyed these four empires? It represented an empire that will never be destroyed. It will last forever. The rock was Jesus Christ, whose kingdom will never end.

The important point to notice about Nebuchadnezzar's dream is that the Lord told Daniel these four empires would cover *all of history* from his own time until the end of the age. Yet the last of these four empires declined and faded away long ago. If the Bible is true, that empire *must* reappear before the end of history. And that's exactly what seems to be happening today, in the form of the European Union.

EMPIRES COME AND GO

The message God sent to Nebuchadnezzar was so important that he gave the same message directly to Daniel in a vision, a revelation from God that enabled him to see future events in symbolic form. In his vision, Daniel saw four fantastic animals coming from the sea. The first animal was a lion-like creature with wings like an eagle's. Second came a lop-sided bear-like animal, raised up on one of its sides and carrying three ribs in its mouth. The third animal looked like a leopard, but had four wings on its back. The fourth animal was different from all the others. It had ten horns and iron teeth. It crushed its victims with its teeth, then devoured them and trampled underfoot whatever was left. While Daniel watched, a small horn came up among the fourth animal's ten horns, uprooting three of them. This little horn had eyes like a man's and a mouth that spoke boastfully. Then, as Daniel looked on, the Lord came in judgment and this final beast was destroyed.

Fortunately, the Lord revealed the meaning of this vision to Daniel, and that explanation is recorded for us in the book of Daniel. It turns out that the four animals, like the four parts of the statue in Nebuchadnezzar's dream, represented four empires. Again, these four empires correspond to the Babylonian, Persian, Greek, and Roman empires. But Daniel was especially interested in the fourth beast, the one showing the Roman Empire. The Lord told him this empire would be unlike any other empire, and would "devour the whole earth, trampling it down and crushing it."[2] The ten horns that Daniel saw represented ten rulers from this empire. The little horn was a coming ruler who would overcome three of those kings.

The Lord went on to tell Daniel six specific facts about this coming world ruler: (1) He will speak against God. (2) He will oppress God's holy people, the Jews. (3) He will try to change the times that God has set. Through the centuries, Satan has tried repeatedly to overthrow God's timing — from the time he tried to wipe out God's people in Egypt to the occasion he tried to have baby Jesus killed by King Herod. This coming world ruler will try the same tactic. (4) He will try to change the laws that

God has established. Again, like Satan, he will try to vie with God Himself for leadership over the world. (5) God's holy people, the Jews, will be handed over to him for three-and-a-half years. This will be the worst period in earth's history. (6) When the Lord comes to earth, this wicked world ruler will be judged and his power will be wiped out. Then the Lord's kingdom will rule the earth, and it will last forever.

So the Bible clearly predicts the career of the coming world ruler. His initial base of operation will be a revived form of the Roman Empire. It will be even more impressive than the original empire, as great as that was. At the climax of history, the Roman Empire will reveal itself as an aggressive, predatory power. Its leader will be a vicious and law-less man. And it will spread its dominion over all the earth.

ANCIENT ROMAN EMPIRE REVIVED

Ever since the Roman Empire fell apart at the beginning of the Middle Ages, people have tried to bring it back. This goal is not surprising. After all, the Roman Empire gave Europe, Asia, and Africa prosperity on a scale that was previously unimagined. The empire was powerful enough to enforce peace throughout the Mediterranean world.

But all the efforts to rebuild the ancient empire were doomed. The Roman Empire had been united by a single language and culture, as well as by a single government. When the empire was broken up into dozens of separate fragments, each piece of the old empire developed its own language and identity. The conflicting cultures, languages, and values of these many nations kept them from unifying. In fact, they spent much of their time and energy fighting each other. Like Humpty Dumpty, the Roman Empire just could not be put back together again.

But attempts to put the Roman Empire back together molded European history. About a thousand years ago, Charlemagne, king of the Franks, built a so-called Roman Empire that lasted a little over one hundred years. But it was nothing like the original. It was much smaller and less powerful. For a few years at the end of the 1800's and the beginning of the 1900's, the Germans ruled the Second Reich, or Second Empire — another attempt to rebuild the Roman Empire. Germany's defeat in World War I destroyed this "Roman" empire. Then German dictator Adolf Hitler conquered much of Europe in the Third Reich — the Third Empire. He proclaimed that this empire would endure for a thousand years. It lasted barely a decade. It was destroyed in the rubble of World War II, and all of Europe was nearly destroyed with it.

Yet today's version of the Roman Empire was born in 1950, just five years after the collapse of Hitler's great attempt to recreate the Roman Empire. And this time, the effort seems to be succeeding. Five years after the end of World War II, Jean Monnet, a Frenchman with the dream of a borderless Europe, proposed a simple step toward unity. He suggested that the European nations create a single market in coal and steel under the control of an independent authority. Germany, Italy, the Netherlands, Belgium and Luxembourg warmly received the proposal.

Seven years later, the Treaty of Rome moved Europe much closer toward a single government. It established the European Economic Community (EEC) and began to set up a central governmental machinery. From that time on, the European Community has been the major axis round which the movement for a united Europe has turned.

In 1963, the EEC took another step toward rebuilding the ancient Roman Empire — it made its first foreign-policy decisions. The countries of the European Union signed a treaty with their former African colonies, guaranteeing them trading advantages and financial aid.

Step by step, Europe has begun acting more like a single country. In 1979, the people of Europe began electing representatives directly to the European Parliament, the EU's governing assembly. The 1992 Treaty on European Union gave the European Community a new name that reflects its goal of creating a single foreign policy, a single security policy, and a single defense policy across Europe. The new name is the European Union — not just an alliance of nations, but a true empire. As Jean Monnet, the father of the EU, put it decades ago, "We are not building a coalition of States, we are uniting people." In January of 2002, many of the citizens of this new empire abandoned their old national monetary systems and adopted a new currency. The Euro, as the new currency is called, was introduced into stores and shops across continental Europe.

Think how unexpected this new European Union is! For over 1500 years, Europe has been split into dozens of nations, jealously guarding their independence. Three great efforts to rebuild the ancient Roman Empire seemed to demonstrate the difficulty in bringing competing nations together. Different languages, cultures, and economic interests divided the territory of the old Roman Empire. Over the past few years, the EU has grown, until now it has well over ten members. The ten horns, or leaders of a united Europe, that Daniel saw in his vision could reveal themselves at any time.

The EU and the Middle East

As the EU has worked to build a single foreign policy, it has become more and more involved in international politics. The EU is especially interested in gaining stability in its own neighborhood — and the Middle East is Europe's back yard. In recent years, several important peace negotiations for Mideast peace have been hosted by Europeans. The Madrid peace talks of 1991 are a prime example. Today, the EU stands alongside the US, Russia, and the United Nations as one of the four great political powers trying to broker a peace between Israel and its Arab enemies.

Since the 9/11 attacks, the EU has taken an even more prominent role in the quest for peace in the

Mideast. Since the EU does not generally see eye-to-eye with the US on the Arab-Israeli conflict, it is not surprising that it has insisted on speaking with its own voice, rather than simply agreeing with American proposals. Over the years, the European Union has had a frosty relationship with Israel and has given support to the Palestinian Authority of terrorist Yasser Arafat. In fact, the EU has been the Palestinian Authority's *greatest* financial backer.

The EU's friendly relationship with the Palestinians and other Arabs may prove useful in the future, when (as the prophet Daniel tells us) Europe's leader will negotiate and establish a peace agreement. Since modern Israel was founded in 1948, Arab hostility and distrust have been the barrier to peace in the Middle East. If the Arab and Muslim nations feel they can trust the Europeans, the EU will have a tremendous advantage over the US, which has traditionally been a strong supporter of Israel.

The tilt that many Europeans have shown in favor of the Arabs has often made them highly critical of the US's peace efforts in the Middle East. In May of 2002, European criticism became so pointed that US Secretary of State Colin Powell retorted, in effect, "Get off our case!" Mr. Powell said, "There are some in Europe who are quick to find fault with any position that the United States might take that we believe is a correct, principled position . . . " For a decade after the fall of the Soviet Union at the beginning of the 1990's, the US has reigned as the world's only superpower. But as a newly united and mighty

Europe gains confidence and asserts its influence, we may well expect the EU to challenge the US's authority in Europe and the Middle East.

THE UNITED STATES IN PROPHECY

But what will happen to the US? If the EU pushes the United States aside in Europe and the Middle East, in what direction will the US move? The Bible tells us what role Europe, Israel, Egypt, and many other nations will play in history's final drama. But what of the US?

Some people, seeing the central place of the US in world affairs during the past one hundred years, have strained to find some mention of this world power in biblical prophecy. But, in fact, the US is not there. For one reason or another, it seems that the US will not play a key role in the seven-year countdown to the return of Jesus Christ. This may be because the US will unite with the EU in taking leadership in the Middle East, which is across the Atlantic from the US, but only a short plane-hop from Europe. The US may also be preoccupied with protecting its own borders against terrorists and with other serious problems closer to home.

Aligned with the EU

The European Union has an economy about as large as the United States' — and a larger population. Its exports exceed those of the US. The EU is an important trading partner with the US, and

Europe and the United States have extensive investments in each other's economies. The US simply cannot afford to ignore the EU's opinions and desires regarding the Mideast peace that all the world's major powers are seeking. In fact, the US may soon tire of European sniping at its long-standing efforts to bring a fair peace to Israel and Palestine and may gladly allow our European allies to assume control over the peace process.

This is especially true now that British Prime Minister Tony Blair, a great friend of the US, has taken a leading role in the effort to bring peace to the Middle East. Not only are the British especially close to the US; they are also members of the EU. The US may rejoice at the chance to pass its baton to the British.

Protecting Our Own Borders

There is also the somewhat remote possibility that America may conclude that friendship with Israel is dangerous. In that scenario as well, the US might leave the resolution of the Mideast crisis to others. The September 11 terrorist attacks shook Americans in a dramatic way, just as the attack on Pearl Harbor and the assassination of President Kennedy affected earlier generations. As of May 2002, the American public's sense of personal security still hadn't returned, reported Michael Traugott of the University of Michigan. "The impact of the attack has been relatively severe and relatively durable," he said.[3]

In addition, the financial impact of 9/11 and ongoing terrorist attempts against the US may compel America to look inward. The US may have to focus on protecting itself. After the 9/11 attacks, the US stock market suffered a huge decline. That isn't surprising. The stock market usually sinks rapidly when a major crisis, such as a war or a presidential assassination, strikes the country. But typically, a year later the market has posted a 25% *gain*. This time around, that isn't happening. 9/11 dealt a serious blow to the US economy.

The economic impact of 9/11 may be compounded by future attacks. US Vice President Dick Cheney has warned, "The prospects of a future attack against the United States" by the al Qaeda terrorist network "are almost certain." This is, he added, "Not a matter of *if*, but *when*." Underscoring the severity of the threat, he said, "It could happen tomorrow; it could happen next week; it could happen next year, but they will keep trying."[4] As the reality of a long-term struggle with hidden enemies strikes home, the economic damage inflicted on the US by the terrorist war may cause future politicians to reconsider America's efforts in the Middle East.

FUTURE OF THE EU

The US is constantly rethinking its role in the Mideast. The way is being cleared for the European Union, as a united empire, to take its place as a superpower. Step by step, the European Union is using its economic power to build its political influence. Remembering a thousand years of constant warfare, capped by two devastating world wars that began in Europe, the EU wants peace and stability in its part of the world. And its part of the world includes Israel, separated from Europe only by the Mediterranean Sea. Europe has a much greater stake in the Mideast peace process than does the US. The EU is already involving itself more and more actively in the Arab-Israeli peace process, and we can expect its contribution to become ever more important.

As the EU intentionally moves toward creating a completely unified Europe, it is beginning to add military muscle to its economic power. At the end of 2001, the EU for the first time established its own military force.[5] That was just a beginning. The EU has a larger population and an economy that could soon challenge the US's economic engine. In the future, the EU may be able to build an army to rival, or even surpass, the US's powerful military forces. The famed Roman legions that conquered and dominated the ancient world may soon return.

A Uniquely Gifted Leader

As we consider the European Union's successful efforts to, in effect, rebuild the great Roman Empire, we might well ask, "What's missing? What's coming next?" The answer, of course, is that the new "Roman Empire" has no *emperor*. Europe is already building herself into a single great union with a single economy, a single currency and a single government. But it does not have a single leader — a popular, highly visible ruler. The kind of leader who can cement the European unity that to this point has been forged mostly by faceless bureaucrats. A leader who can be the worthy focus of European loyalty and patriotism. A Roman emperor.

That's the next logical step. And the Bible tells us that's exactly what's coming. As the previous chapter describes in detail, during earth's coming seven-year judgment, Europe will be led by a uniquely gifted leader who will be able to leverage his leadership of the European continent into a *world* empire. This coming Roman emperor will pose as a man of peace. He will be a great orator. He will be able persuade sworn enemies to sit down together and negotiate. Then he will secure their signatures on a history-making peace agreement.

This brilliant, charismatic, seemingly peaceful man is coming. The world will be ready for him. When he does come, there will be a brief interlude of peace, followed by days filled with terror. This man's leadership will not go unchallenged. As we will see in the next chapter, just when the Middle East peace seems to be working, Russia will gather other nations to invade Israel from the north.

Chapter Seven Endnotes

[1]Daniel 2:38.

[2]Daniel 7:33.

[3]Will Lester, "Terrorist Attacks Shook Americans," seattlepi.com, May 20, 2002 (http://seattlepi.nwsource.com/national/apus_story. asp?category=1110&slug=Attacks%20Attitudes; retrieved May 21,

2002).

[4]*Washington Post*, May 18, 2002.

[5]"EU Military Force Sanctioned," CNN.com/World, December 15, 2001 (http://www.cnn.com/2001/WORLD/europe/12/15/eu.summit. expand/; retrieved June 4, 2002).

CHAPTER 8

THE RUSSIAN INVASION
OF ISRAEL

The Bible tells us that at a time when Israel is at peace and feeling secure in its own land, Russia will swoop down and invade from the north. A few years ago, when the Cold War was raging, it was hard to picture such an invasion. Wouldn't the US retaliate with massive attacks on Russia? But since September 11, 2001, Russia has cultivated a friendship with the United States, as well as with the European Union. At the same time Russia continues to maintain close ties to Islamic countries hostile to Israel. The picture has changed.

AFTER THE COLD WAR

For more than half a century after World War II, the Cold War raged, becoming ever more dangerous as the US and Russia refined their ability to destroy one another. The Cold War influenced the foreign policy of every nation on earth and dominated the military budget of the United States — but Russia drowned in a sea of debt. Russia's economy was much weaker than the US's, and it was poorly managed by its Communist dictators. The overwhelming expense of the military contest with the United States crippled Russia. Its leaders spent huge amounts of money for world conquest, never having to worry about being voted out of office. But the money they spent came from the pockets of Russian workers. In 1956, author John Gunther visited Russia and returned to write a sympathetic account of life there. Yet he noted, "The cruelest thing in the Soviet Union, which helps to make it the cruelest country on earth, is the grisly economic toll it extracts from its citizens."[1] Years later, President Ronald Reagan's label for this cruelest country was "the Evil Empire."

"Mr. Gorbachev, take down this wall!" was President Reagan's demand as he confronted the Berlin Wall, erected to hinder people trying to escape from Communism. Then, in the early 1990's, the Evil Empire fell. The Russian economy cracked under the strain of crippling military costs and Communist mismanagement, and Russia's leaders became friendlier toward the Western nations. At the same time, they opened their ears to ideas of freedom, democracy, and Christianity. Finally, the USSR fractured into no less than a dozen pieces, as Russia freed its neighbors from their satellite status. In December of 1991, US President George Bush declared, "the United States recognizes and welcomes the emergence of a free, independent, and democratic Russia . . . "[2] For the first time in decades, Russia was an open society. The Soviet Empire was history.

These astonishing changes in Russia opened the promise of a new, exciting, and profitable relationship with the United States. Yet in the years immediately after the Evil Empire's fall, much of the optimism evaporated. Despite Western aid, the Russian economy stagnated and deteriorated. Misunderstandings, national pride, and conflicting interests put the US and Russia on opposite sides in political and military conflicts across the globe. In hot spots like Libya, Iraq, Bosnia and Afghanistan, the two nations once again appeared to be on a collision course.

A LASTING FRIENDSHIP WITH AMERICA?

Then, on September 11, 2001, another kind of collision turned that picture completely around. After terrorists crashed airliners into the World Trade Center and the Pentagon, Russian President Vladimir Putin was the first head of state to call and express his sympathy and concern to President Bush. In the months after the attacks, a new friendship grew up between the United States and Russia, reflected in the personal warmth between the two countries' Presidents.

Even before the terrorist attacks, the Russian leader had favorably impressed President Bush. At a meeting in the summer of 2001, Putin explained to

Bush why he always wears a certain cross. His mother apparently gave him the cross when he made a visit to Jerusalem, and while there he had it blessed by a priest at the traditional site of Jesus' tomb. The cross later survived a devastating fire at Putin's summer cottage, from which he had had to rescue his two young daughters. As Putin told the story to television's Larry King, "I was surprised completely when one of the workers, just muddling through those ashes of the remnants, found that cross intact. And the house fell. That was a surprise, a revelation, and therefore I always now keep the cross with me."[3]

Putin "basically seemed like he was saying there was a higher power," the President later told author Peggy Noonan.[4]

It is not surprising that President Bush considers personal faith important for a national leader. He credits Jesus Christ with changing his own life. At a candidates' debate while campaigning for the presidency, he was asked what "political philosopher or thinker" he most identified with. He replied, "Christ, because he changed my heart." Asked to say more, he continued, "When you turn your heart and your life over to Christ, when you accept Christ as Savior, it changes the heart and changes your life, and that's what happened to me."[5]

Since the September 11 attacks, the friendship between the Russian and American leaders has grown closer. In November 2001, President Bush hosted Russia's President Putin at his Texas ranch. The two heads of state clearly enjoyed each other's company as they toured the ranch in Mr. Bush's pickup truck, slapped each other on the back, and joked. President Bush remarked that in Texas "you only invite a good friend to your home." He said, "The more I get to know President Putin, the more I get to see his heart and soul . . . the more I know we can work together in a positive way."[6]

In addition to their personal goodwill, Presidents Bush and Putin doubtless realize that Russia and the US now have common interests. For example, Russia is concerned about attacks by Muslim extremists, such as those in Chechnya who have staged attacks on Russian civilians during the past few years. Some of the foreigners fighting alongside the pro-terrorist Taliban in Afghanistan after 9/11 came from Chechnya. US security now demands that we destroy terrorist cells in Afghanistan, nearly 7,000 miles from our country. The Russian government has every reason to cheer us on. Afghanistan is right in Russia's back yard!

NO FRIEND OF ISRAEL

Despite their new friendship, the US and Russia do not see eye to eye on every issue. Since the foundation of the modern state of Israel in 1948, the US has been that tiny nation's strongest ally. Russia, on the other hand, has supported and armed Israel's enemies. And it continues to do so.

During the Cold War, Russia opposed Israel and aggressively supported several of Israel's bitter Muslim enemies. In the years before Egypt's 1979 peace treaty with Israel, while Egypt was determined to destroy Israel, Russia even sent thousands of its own soldiers to Egypt as military advisers. Today, Russia continues to supply weapons to Muslim countries that are sworn enemies of Israel. These include the rogue governments of Iraq, Iran, Syria, and Libya. Russia has made many positive changes in recent years. But her friendship with the US has not been matched by friendship toward Israel.

The Bible tells us that a ruler from the land to the far north of Israel will lead a marauding force of invaders into the Holy Land. That land is Russia. When the prophesied invasion takes place, Israel will be a nation at peace, secure in its borders, unsuspecting, and completely unprepared for war. The biblical prophets describe just how that unexpected invasion from the far north will play out.

ISRAEL RETURNS TO THE LAND

Writing more than five hundred years before the time of Christ, the prophet Ezekiel foretells the scattering of the people of Israel throughout the world. This prophet also predicts that the Jews will one day be gathered again to their own land. It seems clear that this prophecy began to be fulfilled in 1948 with the establishment of the state of Israel. The Jews had survived nearly 2,000 years without a homeland. Now they had a land of their own again!

Many beautiful and poetic descriptions of Israel's miraculous rebirth have been written. But no celebration of Israel's rebirth approaches the beauty of

Ezekiel's account, written some 2,500 years ago. The Lord took Ezekiel to a valley filled with dry bones and commanded the prophet to prophesy to them.

The prophet did what he was commanded. He preached to the strangest audience ever — a congregation of dry bones! Then, Ezekiel says, "there was a noise, a rattling sound, and the bones came together, bone to bone. I looked, and tendons and flesh appeared on them and skin covered them, but there was no breath in them."[7] Those bones are a portrait of the nation of Israel as we see it today. In fulfillment of this prophecy, the Jews once again control their Promised Land, but many of them are still spiritually dead. There is "no breath in them." Ezekiel predicts that the regathered Jews will one day relax with a sense of peace and safety. But during this time of false security they will be invaded by a coalition of nations led by a leader referred to as Gog. Though this man's headquarters will lie in Russian territory, he will also rule over lands on Russia's border. This leader will govern a powerful empire that may include even more territory than the 20th century "Evil Empire" of the USSR!

THE RUSSIAN-ARAB ALLIANCE

Ezekiel identifies several nations that will be Russia's allies in the coming invasion. His list reads something like a roll call of Israel's current Arab and Muslim enemies! Russia's forces will be accompanied by a great horde that includes Iran, the upper

Nile region, and possibly Libya.[8] The coalition that will help Russia plunder Israel is already substantially in place today. This leader will march down into Israel from the north at the head of a coalition of largely Islamic nations that hate Israel.

If it's true that Russia and its allies are already poised to be Israel's enemies, could the big invasion occur today? Actually, the answer is no. Ezekiel predicts that Russia will invade when Israel is at peace, secure in its borders, and completely unprepared for war. Israel will be at rest, Ezekiel says, without the walls and fences that protect its communities today.

Today, Israel is the most security-conscious nation on earth. It is constantly on the alert against the bitter enemies that surround it. To understand the security challenge Israel faces, we need to remember that Israel's current enemies include not only hostile nations but also homegrown Arab homicide bombers and a global network of fundamentalist Muslim terrorists. Behind Osama bin Laden's hatred for America, for instance, is America's support for Israel. As bin Laden said in a 1998 interview, "We are sure of our victory against the Americans and the Jews as promised by the Prophet . . . The American government, we think, is an agent that represents Israel inside America.[9]

Israel has been forced to defend itself against enemies like this since the day it was reestablished as a nation. It spends more on its national defense per person than any other nation on earth. It is the only country in the world that has to provide gas masks for its entire population! Twice, Ezekiel mentions that when Russia attacks, Israel will be a land without walls. But today, the land is full of security walls and fences, with more being built all the time.

What will prompt Israel to tear down the walls? What will make the Israelis feel they are safe while their country is still encircled by her enemies?

Israel's confidence will probably stem from promises the Antichrist will make as the leader of the revived version of the Roman Empire. The epic peace agreement will be in place, and the massive military power of their nearby neighbors might give the Jews the assurance they need to drop their guard. At this time it is admittedly hard to imagine Israel taking such a step, but the Bible makes it clear — the day is coming; even today some of the key players are in place.

The Israelis may also be reassured by political developments like the new friendship between Russia and the United States. If Russia is an ally of Israel's greatest friend, how could Russia possibly attack them?

As Ezekiel points out, Israel's period of peace and safety will not last for long! Russia and its allies will launch a surprise invasion against it. What will drive the armies of Russia and its allies to move into Israel? And what will become of their plans? Ezekiel tells us the motive for Russia's attack will be economic. Perhaps Russia will see this as a golden opportunity to grab the riches of the rebuilt nation of Israel, just as Russia plundered the Eastern European nations defeated in World War II. And at first, the

Bible says, Russia's attack will overwhelm Israel. "You and all your troops and the many nations with you will go up, advancing like a storm; you will be like a cloud covering the land."[10] Israel will be helpless under the onslaught of a vastly superior force. And the United States, Israel's greatest ally, will not run to Israel's aid.

WHERE'S THE US?

Where will the United States be at this point? Why won't the US crush the Russian invasion? The Bible doesn't say. But there are several possibilities. Perhaps the US will be caught totally by surprise, just as we were on 9/11. The United States may be spread thin in its war against terrorism. It might not be workable for the US to counter Russia and the many nations allied with it. And possibly the US's hands will be tied by an alliance with Russia, growing out of the new friendship that has recently sprouted between the two countries.

Is it even possible the US will do nothing because there will no longer *be* a United States of America as we know it today? That's Osama bin Laden's plan for America! "We predict a black day for America and the end of the United States as United States. It will be separate states, and will retreat from our land and collect the bodies of its sons back to America. Allah willing."[11] Whatever the reason, it is clear from Scripture that the last time around, it will not be the United States that will rush to save Israel.

TURNAROUND

After his first flush of victory, this leader (Gog) from the north will suddenly fall. He will be completely crushed — the Lord Himself will overthrow him. First, He will set the invading forces against each other. "When Gog attacks the land of Israel, my hot anger will be aroused, declares the Sovereign Lord . . . I will summon a sword against Gog on all my mountains, declares the Sovereign Lord. Every man's sword will be against his brother."[12] Further, the Lord will personally go to war against this man, sending plague and bloodshed, torrents of rain and hailstones, and even burning sulfur on him and his troops. Not only will his armies be destroyed in Israel, but the Lord will also take the war home to this leader's Russian base.[13]

The fire the Lord sends looks like a direct judgment from His hand, but it could also refer to the fire of a nuclear attack. If so, Israel itself may launch the bombs that cause this fire. Israel has been a nuclear power for decades now. Or perhaps the United States will finally come to Israel's aid and attack its enemies. Whatever this fire is, the Lord Himself will choose the time and the place where it will fall.

The impact of these divine counter-attacks on the invaders will be devastating. In a detailed account of the aftermath of the great battle between this Russian leader and God, Ezekiel predicts:

- Israelis will gather the invaders' weapons and use them for fuel — for *seven years*: "They will not need to gather wood from the fields or cut it from the forests, because they will use the weapons for fuel."

- One of the mounds of the buried corpses, piled up in a mass grave, will be so large that it will form a barrier to travel.
- The burial of openly visible corpses will require seven months to complete — and then will have to be followed by a systematic search for hidden bodies.

God's purpose in the coming humiliation of Israel's enemy from the north is clear. He says, "I will show my greatness and my holiness, and I will make myself known in the sight of many nations. Then they will know that I am the Lord."[14]

Men who worship a god of their own making, or who worship themselves, will hate Israel and try to plunder it. Perhaps some of the attackers will shout religious slogans as they advance, just as Muslim terrorists today blow up innocent victims with the words "Allah akbar!" (Allah is great) on their lips. Those invaders will learn that it is Jehovah, the God of Israel, who is great. Massive armies are no match for Him. They will learn that *He* is the Lord.

Despite God's direct intervention on Israel's behalf, the nations of the world will soon forget what happened to Russia and her allies. Then, all the nations of the world will send their military forces into Israel for the mother of all battles. The invading armies will be driven by a demonic hatred for Israel. Since 9/11 we have seen the depths of such hatred which seems to intensify with each passing day. We are well on the road to Armageddon — a road paved with militant Islam's desire to eradicate the nation of Israel. In the next chapter we will examine the historical basis for this animosity for the Jews.

Chapter Eight Endnotes

[1] John Gunther, Inside Russia Today (New York: Harper & Brothers, 1957), p. 356.

[2] Raymond L. Garthoff, "US Relations with Russia: The First Five Years," *Current History*, October 1997 (http://www.brook.edu/dybdocroot/views/articles/garthoff/1997ch.htm; retrieved June 4, 2002).

[3] "Putin Talks about Religion with Larry King" (http://www.orthodox.net/russia/2000-09-15-larry-king.html; retrieved June 4, 2002).

[4] Peggy Noonan, *When Character Was King* (New York: Random House, 2001).

[5] "Bush: Faith More Than a Sunday Formality," *USA Today*, July 25, 2000 (http://www.usatoday.com/news/e98/e2248.htm; retrieved June 4, 2002).

[6] Rob Watson, "Bush and Putin 'Best of Buddies,'" BBC News (http://news.bbc.co.uk/hi/english/world/americas/newsid_1659000/1659048.stm; retrieved June 4, 2002).

[7] Ezekiel 37:7,8

[8] Ezekiel 38:5f; for identification of the nations involved, see notes in the *NIV Study Bible*, p. 1280.

[9] ABC News.com, "Talking with Terror's Banker: An Exclusive Interview with Osama bin Laden" (http://abcnews.go.com/sections/world/dailynews/terror_980609.html#targets; retrieved December 4, 2002).

[10] Ezekiel 38:9.

[11] See "Talking with Terror's Banker."

[12] Ezekiel 38:18, 21.

[13] Ezekiel 39:6.

[14] Ezekiel 39:23.

ISLAM AND THE NATIONS VS. ISRAEL

D-Day is coming. One day, the nations of the world, enflamed by demonic hatred, will converge on the land of Israel for the battle of Armageddon. All of earth's armies will gather at this one little dot on the map to do battle. History's greatest drama of human violence and divine judgment will take place in the land that God has called the pupil of His eye.

9/11 and the war against terrorism have fueled a growing hostility and even a hatred for the nation of Israel, setting the stage for this final battle in the Valley of Megiddo.

9/11 AND SINCE — WHY AMERICA WAS ATTACKED

Why did Osama bin Laden attack the US? Self-appointed experts have given all manner of opinions.

Polls show most Americans know exactly why Osama sent jets crashing into American buildings. The US supports Israel. Osama bin Laden, along with millions of other Arabs and Muslims, hates Israel. Osama has made his motives crystal clear via his famous videotapes. In a video broadcast on the day after Christmas in 2001, he said, "Our terrorism is a good, accepted terrorism because it's against America. It's for the purpose of defeating oppression so America will stop its support for Israel, who is killing our children."[1]

Fellow Arabs also know why bin Laden attacked. A month after 9/11, Mayor Rudolph Giuliani of New York rejected a $10 million donation from a Saudi Arabian prince. Why? Because the prince asked for "a more balanced stance towards the Palestinian cause." And what did he think would be "a more balanced" stance? Not protecting *Israel* from the Palestinian *terrorists*, but protecting the *terrorists* from *Israel* — "Our Palestinian brethren continue to be slaughtered at the hands of Israelis while the world turns the other cheek."[2]

Osama bin Laden attacked America because it supports Israel. Israel is the issue. And as history moves toward the fulfillment of biblical prophecy, Israel is becoming the issue *worldwide*. We live in ominous times.

Just as he has told us the *motive* for his attacks, Osama bin Laden has not kept the *purpose* of his September 11 attacks a secret. He intends to destroy America, the greatest obstacle to his plans for Muslim conquest. He longs to relive the early days of Islam, when the prophet Muhammad personally led his warriors in the slaughter of the "heretics." Since the US is still standing, it may look as though Osama's plans have failed. But they have not failed *completely*. Osama has succeeded in upsetting the stability of the world. He has, in effect, knocked the earth off-balance.

We might have expected the world to respond to 9/11 by taking a strong stand against Osama bin Laden's kind of Islam. His vicious attacks show that there is no limit to the evil and radical deeds he perpetrates. But in fact, the opposite has often happened. Many governments hope to avoid trouble not by *opposing* the Muslim extremists, but rather by *appeasing* them. As a result, in many ways the world since 9/11 has become a colder place for the US and Israel, the two nations Osama hates.

GROWING HOSTILITY TOWARD ISRAEL

When the 9/11 attacks struck New York, Washington, and Pennsylvania, many Israelis thought, "*Now* they will understand what life is like for us every day!" Israel could use some genuine empathy. It has been more seriously undermined and weakened by terrorists than has any other nation in today's world. But that understanding has not been forthcoming. Instead, since 9/11 life has become *more difficult* for Israelis. As the US and Europe have scrambled to secure their own borders and fight far-off wars, they have often had *less* time and energy to devote to Israel and its troubles than they did before confronting terrorism.

The war on terrorism has actually brought *greater* hostility toward Israel, because Israel has accepted at face value the claim that the world is at war with terrorists. As a result, Israel has taken this as a "green light" to hunt down the terrorists operating in its vicinity. Some of the Muslim nations who have joined America's anti-terrorist coalition have, in turn, become all the more resentful of Israel. They are willing to admit that the destruction of the World Trade Center was a terrorist act, but they don't call it *terrorism* when someone blows up Jewish families in Israel. To them, the Israelis have no right to defend themselves.

ISRAEL BLAMED FOR THE 9/11 ATTACKS

It seems incredible that anyone could keep a straight face while condemning Israel for trying to *stop* terrorist attacks. How are the Israelis supposed to respond to the efforts to wipe them out — pin bull's eyes on themselves? The kinship Arab and Muslim nations feel toward Palestinian gunmen and homicide bombers is just one evidence of how great is the hatred of the Jews. Here are some other indicators.

Many Muslims have actually convinced themselves that *Israel* planned the 9/11 terrorist attacks. On the very day of the attacks, before any information was available, Arab governments already began issuing communiqués claiming that Israel was to blame. No need to wait for evidence; Israel is always to blame!

In Pakistan, newspapers were replete with fabricated stories claiming that on September 11, many Jews skipped work at the World Trade Center because they had been forewarned of the attacks. Hundreds of Jews died in the destruction of the World Trade Center. But many Muslims see Israel as the root of all evil. The twentieth-century German dictator Adolf Hitler planned to kill all the Jews in the world. He said, "the personification of the devil as the symbol of all evil assumes the living shape of the Jew."[3] Today, many Muslims share this twisted point of view. There are Muslims who are willing to blame Israel for every evil under the sun.

This knee-jerk hatred of Israel is so common among Muslims that their leaders can make ridiculous and false accusations against Israel, which are considered fact on the "Arab Street." In January of 2002, for example, Israeli commandos caught a ship smuggling illegal arms from Iran to the Palestinians. But Palestinian Liberation Organization's chairman, Yasser Arafat, claimed that it was, in fact, *Israel* behind the smuggling! Arafat did not say this in order to influence world opinion. The world knows that Arafat's own right-hand lieutenant arranged the shipment. His words were for popular consumption in the Arab world. He was addressing ordinary Muslim men and women, schooled in the hatred of Israel and ready to swallow any lie about Israel. One cannot understand the Arab-Israeli conflict without making a careful examination of the mindless hatred many Arabs have for Israel.

ANTI-SEMITISM AROUND THE WORLD

On September 11, 2001, Muslims in the Palestinian territories and elsewhere around the world rejoiced over the sudden death of thousands of innocent people. In the following days, thousands of Muslims across the globe loudly expressed their support and admiration for Osama bin Laden. Some were worried that the reaction might be serious outbreaks of violence against the Muslims, themselves. They should have known better. The truth is, since 9/11 there *has* been a great deal of violence across Europe — not against Muslims, but against *Jews*. For example, in France, hundreds of anti-Jewish incidents have been reported in recent months.[4]

Similarly, the United Nations has taken an especially harsh stance toward Israel since 9/11. The UN has long treated Israel as a second-class member.[5] After 9/11, we might expect the UN to show some sympathy toward this nation that has suffered even more from terrorism than the US. Instead, since the tragedy, the UN has been explicitly *hostile* toward Israel's fight against terrorism. During Israel's "Operation Defensive Wall" anti-terrorist sweep, authorities discovered hard evidence that personally linked Palestinian President Yasser Arafat to these terrorist attacks.[6] Yet UN Secretary General Kofi Annan's anger was directed not at Arafat, but at Israel. Annan went so far as to claim the whole world was demanding that Israel withdraw.

Most nations of the world have shown surprisingly little outrage at the Islamic indoctrination that inspired their people to commit these attacks. The international community has rarely confronted the Muslim nations who teach their children bigoted, anti-Jewish values. It has become a case of blaming the victim, namely Israel. And as long as the US stands beside Israel, these nations will attempt to make life as difficult as possible for America, as well.

THE ROOTS OF ARAB HOSTILITY

Millions of Muslims from the far corners of the world hate the Jews. Why do they harbor such hatred? What is the source, the origin, and the rationale for this malignant hostility?

The rage that Israel's neighbors show toward this little nation has roots that can be traced to the early chapters of biblical history. Much of the hostility harks back to an ancient family quarrel that has never been resolved. Both the Jews and the Arabs are blood descendants of the biblical patriarch Abraham. The Jews are Abraham's progeny through his son, Isaac. Subsequently, God renamed Jacob, Isaac's son, "Israel." The Jews are Israel's (Jacob's) descendants. Another son of Abraham, named Ishmael, is the father of most of the Arab peoples.

So, both the Jews and the Arabs possess a legitimate claim to being Abraham's descendants. Even before Isaac and Ishmael were born, God predicted that they would take different paths and live as enemies.

Let's see how this happened.

The story began when God called Abraham from his Mesopotamian home in what is today Iraq. He told Abraham to go to the land He would show him, greater Palestine. While Abraham was living as a foreigner in ancient Palestine, the Lord gave him a promise. He said that He would make of Abraham's descendants a great nation and would give them the land in which Abraham was living. It is well to note that the terms "Land of Israel" and "Land of Palestine" have traditionally, and for all practical purposes, been synonymous terms. The identification of Palestine as detached from Israel is of modern origin. More recent events have made a great "separation" in the use of these terms.

But here the plot thickens. Abraham welcomed God's promise and wanted to see it come to pass. But Abraham and his wife, Sarah, were elderly and childless. In fact, Sarah was well past childbearing age, so Abraham and Sarah tried to work out God's promise by their own methods. Sarah sent Hagar, her Egyptian handmaiden, to Abraham's bed in order to have a child by Abraham. Legally, the child would be Sarah's because Hagar was but a servant and therefore, a "surrogate" mother.

Hagar did indeed bear a son, named Ishmael. But he was *not* the son God had promised to Abraham. Before Ishmael's birth, the Lord described the kind of person he would be. "He will be a wild donkey of a man; his hand will be against everyone and everyone's hand against him, and he will live in hostility toward all his brothers."[7] The descendant God had promised Abraham came thirteen years later. Again,

God described his life before he was born. "Your wife Sarah will bear you a son, and you will call him Isaac. I will establish my covenant with him as an *everlasting* covenant for his descendants after him."[8]

So Abraham's oldest son, who would normally inherit his father's estate, was not given the rights of a firstborn son. And the younger son, Isaac, inherited all the privileges of a firstborn son, which included God's promise of the land of Israel. The two half brothers became enemies. Eventually, Ishmael was thrown out of the house. This was a foretaste of things to come. Just as God prophesied that Ishmael would be a "wild donkey of a man" who would "live in hostility toward all his brothers," so the Bible reports that Ishmael's sons "lived in hostility toward all their brothers."[9] And chief among those brothers was Isaac, the ancestor of the Jews. It seems quite evident that Ishmael's "wild-donkey" mentality is at work among some of his descendants in the Middle East.

ISAAC VS. ISHMAEL

God promised the land of Israel to Isaac's sons, the Jews — not to the Arabs, who are for the most part Ishmael's offspring. But more is at issue here than a little slice of land that holds fewer people than some American cities. Much more is at stake. Not only did God promise Abraham that his descendants would own the land of Israel; He also promised that one of his descendants would save the world. "All peoples of the earth will be blessed through you,"

God said. He was talking about Jesus Christ, His unique Son.

Why did God choose the Jews as His special people? Why did God promise Israel a land that stretches across the entire Fertile Crescent from the River of Egypt to the Tigris and Euphrates River valleys of Iraq? The poet Ogden Nash wrote,

> How odd
> Of God
> To choose
> The Jews

This little rhyme may sound disrespectful. But it actually echoes God's own words. "The Lord did not set His affection on you because you were more numerous than other peoples, for you were the fewest of all peoples. But it was because the Lord loved you . . . "[10] God did not choose the Jews because they were greater or more impressive than other nations. His choice was an expression of his *grace* — freely offered. One might say it was favor, lavishly bestowed.

Many of those who best understand God's promises to Abraham are convinced that they are *unconditional* promises. They cannot be undone by anything the Jews may do or not do. They have not been cancelled because the Jews have largely rejected Jesus Christ as their Messiah. People change, and even His beloved people Israel have proven to be fickle and faithless toward Him. God does not change His mind, even when His chosen people do. Many evangelical Bible scholars were not surprised, fifty-plus years ago, to witness the nation of Israel come into existence again after nearly two thousand years of world exile. Such Bible students are convinced that the time will soon come when the nation of Israel will receive Jesus Christ as their Messiah, when He comes to earth for the second time. This is sometimes called Christ's "Second Advent."

Until that time, some wild donkeys will live in hostility toward Israel.

ISLAMIC HATRED FOR ISRAEL

The ancient family feud between Isaac and Ishmael is the oldest source of today's anti-Jewish bigotry, but it is not the only source. Since the seventh century AD, Arab hostility toward the Jews has been compounded by Islamic hatred toward Israel's religion.

First of all, Muslims claim vociferously that *Ishmael*, not Isaac, inherited God's promises to Abraham. Their conclusion, therefore, is that *Ishmael*, not Isaac, is the true owner of the land we today call Israel. They know that this is the opposite of what the Bible says, but they have never had any hesitation in contradicting the Bible. This false Muslim claim that Ishmael's descendants, not the Jews, are the rightful possessors of the land of Israel continues to fuel the Arab-Jewish conflict.

Muslim hostility toward the Jews burst into flames at the very beginning of Islam, when

Muhammad slaughtered unarmed Jewish opponents. According to an ancient Muslim tradition, Muhammad said,

> The last hour will not come before the Muslims fight the Jews and the Muslims kill them, so that Jews will hide behind stones and trees and the stone and the tree will say, "O Muslim, O servant of God! There is a Jew behind me; come and kill him." The only exception will be the box-thorn, for it is one of the trees of the Jews.[11]

The Koran also states, "O you who believe, do not take Jews and Christians as allies; these are allies of one another. Those among you who ally themselves with these belong with them. Allah does not guide the transgressors."[12] The term transgressors obviously refers to Jews and Gentiles. The depth of hatred for Israel seems unimaginable until we understand it is sourced in the one who seeks to murder, rob, steal and destroy.

SATANIC OPPOSITION

Arabs and Muslims display a particularly virulent hatred toward Israel. Behind the scene lurks the author of all hatred. Satan opposes God's plan, which has Israel as its centerpiece. So Satan is determined to wipe out the Jews. Again and again, throughout history, he has almost succeeded. He has used wicked men from many lands to accomplish his plans. 3500 years ago, the Pharaoh of Egypt thought he could destroy the Jews in one generation by killing all their baby boys. A thousand years later, still in biblical times, a Persian official named Haman was less patient. He launched a plan to destroy thousands of Jews by the sword in the space of a single day. He very nearly succeeded.

In AD 70, the Romans destroyed the nation of Israel and drove the Jews out of their land, as the Bible had prophesied. The Jews were scattered in all directions, and remained a persecuted minority in almost every country in which they sought refuge. In medieval England, for example, Jews were forced to wear yellow badges to set them apart from the rest of society. Eventually, in 1290, they were expelled from the British Isles and were not allowed back into England until 1655.

In the middle of the twentieth century, the German dictator Adolf Hitler devised a scheme for wiping every Jew off the face of the earth. He called it "The Final Solution," and in his attempt to carry out this plan he killed as many as six million innocent men, women, and children. Their only crime was that they were Jews.

Today, many Muslims fervently pray and look forward to the day when "the Muslims fight the Jews and the Muslims kill them." Palestinian homicide bombers usually attack innocent Israeli civilians, not military targets. Muslim clerics encourage terrorists like Osama bin Laden in quoting the prophet Muhammad's promise of the coming slaughter of the Jews.

But God has never let such genocide happen. He never will. He has other plans for Israel and the Jews — plans for good. But those plans will not come to pass until the dreams of history's Jew-haters almost come to pass. When the Lord Jesus returns to rescue the Jewish people, the bloody dreams of Pharaoh, Haman, Hitler, and Osama will be thwarted forever.

THE MOTHER OF ALL BATTLES

Today, the eyes of the world are on Israel. Referring to the present Israeli-Palestinian war, British Foreign Office Minister Peter Hain has said, "This is most dangerous conflict in the world and could engulf the region and draw us all in with serious consequences."[13] Mr. Hain is right. But the Bible tells us that the day will come when the conflict in the Middle East will engulf not just that region, but the entire world.

Each murderous rampage in Israel should remind us that God said there would be hostility between the descendants of Isaac and the descendants of Ishmael. The current dispute over the land is deeply rooted in the promises God made to each of these men. Why, after thousands of years, is this now the pre-eminent issue for modern day civilization? In a word, God is positioning the world for a time of judgment and the fulfillment of His commitment to Israel.

The next time a reporter announces another bombing attack of innocent civilians in Israel, remember what God said about the hostility that would exist between brothers. Then remember the yet future carnage He also foretold. Hatred between brothers has become hatred between nations. One day the other nations will attack Israel from every direction. What will ignite this final battle, the War of Armageddon? As we will see in the next chapter, it could be someone like the King of Terrorism — Saddam Hussein.

Chapter Nine Endnotes

[1]"New Osama bin Laden Video Contains Anti-Israel and Anti-American Statements," Anti-Defamation League Online (http://www.adl.org/terrorism_america/bin_l.asp; retrieved June 4, 2002).

[2]Jennifer Steinhauer, "Citing Comments on Attack, Giuliani Rejects Saudi's Gift," *The New York Times*, New York Region, October 12, 2001 (http://www.nytimes.com/2001/10/12/nyregion/12PRIN.html, 020118).

[3]Adolf Hitler, *Mein Kampf*, vol. 1, ch. 11 (see http://www.storm-front.org/books/mein_kampf/mkv1ch11.html; retrieved June 4, 2002).

[4]David A. Harris, "The Virus of Antisemitism Strikes in France," *Forward*, April 12, 2002 (http://www.forward.com/issues/2002/02.04.12/oped1.html; retrieved June 4, 2002).

[5]"Israel and the United Nations," Anti-Defamation League Online (http://www.adl.org/international/Israel-UN-1-introduction.html; retrieved June 4, 2002).

[6]Julie Stahl, "'Terror Invoice' Links Arafat To Terrorism, Expert Says," crosswalk.com/News and Culture (http://news.crosswalk.com/partner/Article_Display_Page/0,,PTID74088%7CCHID194343%7C CIID1132698,00.html; retrieved June 4, 2002).

[7] Genesis 16:12

[8] Genesis 17:19

[9] Genesis 25:17,18

[10] Deuteronomy 7:7,8

[11]"Why Can't the Jews and Muslims Live Together in Peace?" (http://www.islam-qa.com/QA/1%7CBasic_Tenets_of_Faith

(Aqeedah)/Al-Walaa'_wal-Baraa'_(Alliance_and_Amity,_ Disavowal_and_Enmity)/Why_can't_the_Jews_and_Muslims_live_to gether_in_peace.30011999.1098.shtml; retrieved June 4, 2002).

[12]Koran 5:51.

[13]"Operation Protective Wall 3/4/02," BBC News (http://news. bbc.co.uk/hi/english/audiovideo/programmes/newsnight/archive/news id_1917000/1917150.stm; retrieved June 4, 2002).

CHAPTER 10

SADDAM HUSSEIN:
THE KING OF TERRORISM

The Bible predicts that the City of Babylon, which is located in Iraq, will become the centerpiece of Arab unity and the headquarters for an attempt at global dominance. Saddam Hussein, who has quietly been rebuilding Babylon, has embraced terrorism as a means to unify the Arab world against Israel.

AN UNLIKELY KING

While addressing a meeting of the Iraqi National Assembly, the President noticed one member passing a note to another. He immediately pulled out his pistol and, in the middle of his speech, shot the two men. Both died on the spot.[1] The year was 1982, three years after Saddam Hussein had become President of Iraq. Hussein assumed that the note-passers were plotting to assassinate him.

Saddam was no longer the poor boy from the village of Al Awja. The boy who didn't learn to read until he was ten. The boy who stole chickens so his family could eat. He had come a long way. As a young political operative for the Iraqi Ba'th Party, Hussein had wandered through his colleagues' offices, praising the Communist tyrant, Josef Stalin, and insisting that some day he would run Iraq Stalin's way. His listeners used to laugh him off. They shouldn't have. Now his dream has come true.[2]

WHO IS SADDAM HUSSEIN?

Born in 1937, Saddam Hussein joined the revolutionary Ba'th Party as a teenager. The party aims to unite all the world's Arab nations under a single socialist government. Working his way up through the ranks, Hussein quickly became the country's number-two man when the Ba'th party violently overthrew Iraq's government in 1968. Finally, in 1979, Hussein muscled out the nation's leader and took over the government. He soon confirmed that he intended to hold on to power. Making himself a virtual object of worship in Iraq, Hussein plastered the country with twenty-foot-high portraits of himself. To this day, Saddam Hussein retains a stable of full-time artists whose sole responsibility is to craft the heroic renderings of him that appear everywhere in Iraq.

But Saddam does not simply rely on artwork to maintain his hold on power. His old hero, Stalin, is infamous as one of history's great murderers. Similarly, Saddam has earned the title "the Butcher of Baghdad" for his brutal suppression of dissent and his imprisonment, torture, and killing of his enemies, real and imaginary. Aware of the strong family bonds that mold Arab society, he often wipes out the entire family or clan of someone who crosses him.[3] At the same time, however, his energetic quest for Arab unity has made him a hero to Arabs outside his country. Even after the disastrous Gulf War of 1990-91, in which Hussein's unprovoked attack on neighboring Kuwait led his country to a humiliating defeat at the hands of a thirty-three-nation coalition, an Arab commentator remarked, "Saddam Hussein is now the only Arab leader who has a following outside his own country."[4] Many Arabs appreciate Hussein's fierce Arab nationalism and his willingness to stand up to the dominant Western countries.

In pursuit of his heady vision of Arab power, Hussein has been developing weapons of mass destruction — nuclear, chemical, and biological weapons. And there is no doubt he is willing to use these gruesome weapons. Unfortunately for the world's safety, his program has met with some remarkable successes. During the 1990-91 Gulf War, Iraqi forces armed bombs and warheads with deadly biological agents such as anthrax and botulinum toxin. They even aimed Scud missiles outfitted with biological weapons at cities in Saudi Arabia and Israel. Some observers suggest the reason Iraq did not actually fire these weapons was that the US threatened to retaliate with nuclear weapons.[5]

Mustard gas has been illegal in international warfare since it was used with horrible results in World War I, but the ruthless Hussein has even used it on his own people.[6]

Today, Hussein has weapons capable of inflicting massive and indiscriminate destruction on entire civilian populations. And he is willing to use them — even eager to use them. Such determination makes Saddam Hussein the King of Terror. No wonder US President George W. Bush, in his January 2002 State of the Union address, identified Saddam's Iraq as part of the "axis of evil" with North Korea and Iran! Is it possible that frightening and illegal weapons of mass destruction (like those now found in Saddam Hussein's laboratories) may play a significant role in the waves of devastation that will mark the climax of human history? Saddam, and other men like him, may today be perfecting tactics and writing field manuals for tomorrow's apocalyptic battles.

ARAB UNITY

Saddam, the King of Terror, may also be paving the way into the future with his dreams of Arab unity and Arab power, fueled by Arab oil. At a time when the US's dependence on Middle Eastern oil has increased,[7] Iraq holds more than 100 billion barrels of oil, the world's second-largest proven reserve.[8] Saddam's country may also hold the key to a great end-time battle predicted in the Bible.

The Bible identifies the king of the South, or Egypt, as one of the four major international powers during the coming time of destruction called the tribulation. The other major powers will lie to the north of Israel, to Israel's east, and within the territory of the ancient Roman Empire. The Bible's description of these powers suggests the northern power will have its headquarters within the boundaries of the former Russian Empire. The eastern power, with an army of two hundred million soldiers, will presumably include China. Saddam's tireless efforts to build a unified Arab world may soon bear fruit in the biblical "king of the south." This will be a united Arab bloc with its official headquarters in Egypt. In joining Iraq, other Arab nations may prefer a capital in Egypt, a poor country, to keep Iraq's power and wealth from overwhelming the influence of the other members.

If and when it appears, this great Arab confederacy will immediately become a world-dominating force. Controlling most of earth's oil supply, the allies of the "king of the south" will wield political leverage far beyond that of todays powerful but fragmented Organization of Petroleum Exporting Countries (OPEC). And the group's leader, the king of the south, will be able to translate his immense oil revenues into military power. No wonder the Bible portrays Egypt and its allies as capable of launching a major military offensive into the Middle East.

In a world where dictators like Saddam Hussein destabilize long-standing coalitions and pressure their neighbors to abandon centuries-old loyalties, it is difficult to forecast just how the great military powers of the tribulation period will align. We can say, however, that in today's world such alliances can take shape within days, if not hours. At the beginning of the 1990's, no one predicted that the world's oldest and most extreme fundamentalist Muslim country, Saudi Arabia, would join with the United States in a war against another Muslim nation, Iraq. But when Saddam Hussein invaded Kuwait, this coalition formed immediately. And who would have expected that this military alliance would continue into the beginning of the following millennium with a campaign against Afghanistan, another nation controlled by Muslim fundamental-ists? Yet it did. Our era of instability and ever-shift-ing loyalties should seem familiar to readers of George Orwell's novel *1984*, in which public speak-ers had to be prepared to reverse political loyalties in the middle of a speech.

In fact, an often overlooked geographical detail raises a surprising possibility — in history's final hour Iraq may be at the center of a coalition even more significant than Egypt's confederacy. The Antichrist may rule the world from Iraq. The neglected geographical detail? The ancient city of Babylon, site of the tower of Babel and symbol of humanity's rebellion against God, lies in Iraq. And the book of Revelation tells us that at the end of time this city will rule "over the kings of the earth"[9] — and then will be suddenly overthrown.

THE CITY OF BABYLON

Since Babylon is far from being a prosperous

city, many Bible students find it hard to see how this city could be the future capital of the world. Some of them believe that the "Babylon" of the last days will actually be the city of Rome, which is very much alive. But the Old Testament also predicts Babylon's destruction, and it is obviously talking about the city in Iraq. And it seems clear that the destruction of Babylon promised in the Old Testament has not yet taken place. The Old Testament prophets tell us that Babylon will be destroyed suddenly, and then no one will ever live there — no one will even travel through the city! [10] And once this desolation occurs, the city will never be rebuilt.[11] But Babylon has *not* been suddenly destroyed. Through the centuries, people have continued to live in Babylon. And today travelers regularly pass through Babylon.

Babylon's current state of "ruin" came about gradually, as the center of world power moved westward. But centuries after the supposed "destruction" of Babylon, thousands of people lived there and major construction projects were undertaken. The great conqueror Alexander the Great moved to Babylon, planning to make it the capital of his world empire. Before he had the opportunity to realize his dream, he died — in Babylon. Later rulers continued construction of the Greek theater that Alexander began building at his new capital. In the ninth and tenth centuries AD, Babylon was the capital of a Muslim province named *Babel*.[12]

The Old Testament prophesies that Babylon will be "a place where no one lives."[13] Clearly, that prophecy has not yet been fulfilled. What about the prophecy that Babylon will be a land "through which no man travels?"[14] If that prophecy has already come true, the news will come as a bitter disappointment to the proprietors of the Babylon Tourist Hotel and other establishments that cater to the tourists who visit Babylon. Actually located on the site of ancient Babylon, this forty-one-room motel boasts air conditioning, central heating, color TV, room service, health club, sauna, and a game room for the kids. Cost per night — about thirty-five to forty-five dollars. While visiting Babylon, the visitor can dine at any of several restaurants, including the Al Zayiton, the Al Buydir, and the Al Sayab restaurant (perhaps the best of the lot).[15]

If the Bible's prophecies of Babylon's sudden and final destruction have not been fulfilled by now, does that mean that they will never be fulfilled — that the Bible is wrong? Hardly. If the Bible tells us that Babylon will be destroyed in this way, we can be assured that it will happen exactly as predicted. That means Babylon will be rebuilt, becoming once again the queen of earth's cities. In view of the world's rapidly accelerating race toward its midnight hour, we can expect this rebuilding is on its way.

In fact, the rebuilding of Babylon has already begun. That brings us back to the King of Terror, Saddam Hussein.

THE LURE OF BABYLON

King Nebuchadnezzar felt it. He felt the lure of Babylon — the urge to build a world empire with

Babylon as its capital. He became ruler of the known world of his time. As you will recall from our previous discussion, he created the first of the four great world empires that the Bible tells us will dominate world events from Nebuchadnezzar's own time until Christ returns to earth. Nebuchadnezzar built Babylon into a magnificent capital. So magnificent was the city, in fact, that one day, while walking on the roof of the royal palace, Nebuchadnezzar asked himself, "Is not this the great Babylon I have built as the royal residence, by my mighty power and for the glory of my majesty?"[16] God humbled Nebuchadnezzar for the arrogance in this statement, afflicting the king with madness and driving him into the fields, where for seven years he ate grass like an ox. But the Lord did not destroy Babylon's glory. Not yet.

King Cyrus felt it. He felt the lure of Babylon. Cyrus was the ruler of Persia, the second of earth's four great global kingdoms, when he conquered Babylon, as prophesied in the Bible. It was normal in the ancient world for conquerors to destroy the cities they overthrew, but Cyrus did not destroy Babylon. Instead, he elevated it to a royal residence and strengthened the city's fortifications.[17]

Alexander the Great, the founder of the third world Empire, experienced the same urge. After conquering all the lands around him, the Greek ruler chose Babylon as the capital of his vast domain. He provided for the upkeep of the city's traditional pagan holy sites and planned to rebuild the infamous tower of Babel, which through the millennia had fallen into disrepair.[18] After the great flood, God instructed men to spread abroad and fill the earth. Instead, they decided to stick together and build a tower "that reaches to the heavens" so that they could make a name for themselves and achieve glory on their own.[19] The Lord did not allow them to complete their ambitious building project. He divided the laborers into different language groups that could not understand each another. In confusion, the various groups wandered off to settle in different parts of the earth. Alexander wanted to rebuild the tower that so perfectly symbolizes humanity's efforts to achieve permanence and greatness apart from God. The sovereign Lord of heaven and earth did not allow this. Alexander died before he was able to reconstruct that ancient symbol of man's rebellion against God. But some of his other construction plans were continued under later Greek rulers of Babylon.[20] And the lure of Babylon lives on.

THE REBUILDING OF BABYLON

Saddam Hussein feels it. He, too, feels the urge to restore Babylon into a symbol of his own glory and power. And he has begun to do something about it. Over the objections of scientists who abhor the wrecking of a priceless archaeological site, he has begun to destroy Babylon's ancient ruins and rebuild the city. Among other structures, Nebuchadnezzar's southern palace, his throne room, the city's central procession street, and many ancient temples have reappeared.[21] When he built up Babylon for the first time, King Nebuchadnezzar had his own name stamped on the bricks so that future generations could read it and wonder at his magnificence. Saddam Hussein does not want people to overlook any parallels between Nebuchadnezzar the Great and Saddam the Great. Stamped on each of the more than sixty million bricks used in Hussein's rebuilding project at Babylon is the message "Rebuilt in the era of our President Saddam Hussein."[22] Iraq's severe financial troubles since the 1990-91 Gulf War have hindered the completion of Saddam Hussein's grand plan, but the King of Terror still senses the lure of Babylon.

Saddam Hussein clearly feels a deep kinship with Nebuchadnezzar, his ancient predecessor in Babylon. Hussein's numerous portraits attempt to underscore and accentuate his physical resemblance to the ancient king. Why would a modern Muslim ruler try so vigorously to associate his rule with that of an ancient pagan king? One reason, of course, is that Babylon is a great and famous city that just happens to lie within the borders of the nation Saddam Hussein rules. For similar reasons, the Egyptian government sometimes tries to borrow some of the grandeur of the ancient pharaohs. But that is not the entire story. There are other factors at work here that help us understand why, for thousands of years, Babylon has had a strong attraction for world rulers and their imitators.

First, Nebuchadnezzar was ruler of the world. Today, Hussein dreams of a strong, unified Arab nation that will similarly dominate the world.

Further, King Nebuchadnezzar holds pride of place among the elite club of world rulers. You will recall that, though his global empire was smaller and more short-lived than any of the three empires succeeding it, the Bible describes Nebuchadnezzar's Babylonian empire as an empire of *gold* in contrast to the less precious silver, bronze, and iron that described the later empires. The rulers of later empires faced various limitations on their power, but Nebuchadnezzar reigned absolute, supreme. Saddam Hussein is an egomaniac who, in the very least, yearns to be the supreme leader of an Arab confederation.

Another reason for Saddam Hussein to admire King Nebuchadnezzar is that the Babylonian king conquered Jerusalem. He is famed in the Bible and in history as the man who destroyed the Jewish nation. Saddam Hussein harbors a rabid hatred for the Jewish people and the restored nation of Israel that was established in 1948 as a homeland for them. It has been difficult for us in the West to realize how intense and unthinking this anti-Jewish obsession is among some Arabs. But since September 11, 2001, we have begun to get the picture. We discussed the reasons for this hostility in the last chapter. Just as the Bible predicted, this extreme hatred continues to our day. The King of Terror would love to go down in history as the man who, like Nebuchadnezzar, destroyed the nation of Israel.

At the very end of history as we know it, leaders will still feel the lure of Babylon. The Antichrist will be the last of the great world rulers to sense the urge to turn Babylon into the capital of a world empire built on the idea of man's greatness — a greatness apart from God. The Antichrist, or another end-time leader who rules Babylon for a little while[23] before him, will exercise power in a Babylon that is "the great city that rules over the kings of the earth."[24] Ironically, the Antichrist will then turn against Babylon and help destroy it.[25] This final ruler will not hesitate to devastate a towering, obscenely wealthy metropolis, one of the earth's premier cities. Perhaps he will sense that his true base of power lies far to the west, in the heart of the old Roman Empire. The ultimate reason for the decision to overthrow Babylon will lie not in the Antichrist's heart, but in God's plan for the earth.[26] Throughout mankind's final rebellion, God will make certain that His purposes are being fulfilled.

THE CITY OF MAN VS. THE CITY OF GOD

Ever since men erected the tower of Babel as a testimony to their own greatness, Babylon has been the *city of man*. It is the city of man's own glory, man's power, man's ability, and man's freedom from responsibility. In short, it is the city of man's revolt against God's authority. And the Bible tells us that at the end of history a rebellious world will unite, with this city at its center, to make war on Jerusalem, God's holy city!

It is as if, in our day, the world has come full circle. We have traveled the road from creation to the prospect of annihilation. The nation of Israel has emerged from obscurity to international prominence.

We have also journeyed from Isaac and Ishmael to the current day Israeli-Arab conflict. The demise of the Roman Empire has given rise to the EU. Twenty-five hundred years ago there was Nebuchadnezzar; now we have Saddam Hussein. It appears that the final chapter is being written right before our eyes.

The notion of a rebuilt and powerful Babylon sounded absurd just decades ago. Only a few Bible scholars, and perhaps a scheming young politician named Saddam Hussein, considered such a transformation possible. Today, Babylon is poised to take its prophetic role. Saddam Hussein's actions and policies are custom-made to move us toward the coming time when Babylon will rule the world. God Almighty is able to use an evil man like Saddam Hussein to move the world closer to the return of Jesus Christ. In fact, God is using the evil perpetrated on 9/11 to advance His plan and to demonstrate how much we need "The Prince of Peace," Jesus Christ. But that brings us to a critical question. Who is Jesus Christ? Will the One who returns be merely a prophet, as Islam claims, or will He be the Son of God, as Christianity believes? We will find out in the next chapter.

Chapter Ten Endnotes

[1]Daniel Pipes, review of Efraim Karsh and Inari Rautsi , *Saddam Hussein: A Political Biography* (http://www.danielpipes.org/reviews/19910809.shtml; retrieved June 3, 2002).

[2]"Secrets of His Life and Leadership," Frontline, interview with Said K. Aburish, 2000 (http://www.pbs.org/wgbh/pages/frontline/shows/saddam/interviews/aburish.html; retrieved May 30, 2002).

[3]"Secrets of His Life and Leadership."

[4]"Secrets of His Life and Leadership."

[5]"Saddam Spills Secrets," *Time*, December 4, 1995.

[6]"Secrets of His Life and Leadership."

[7]John K. Cooley, "The Oil Outlook for 2002," abcNews.com (http://abcnews.go.com/sections/world/DailyNews/oiloutlook020102_cooley.html; retrieved May 30, 2002). (http://abcnews.go.com/sections/world/DailyNews/oiloutlook020102_cooley.html).

[8]"Iraq," US Department of Energy (http://www.eia.doe.gov/emeu/cabs/iraq.html; retrieved June 4, 2002).

[9]Revelation 17:18.

[10]Jeremiah 51:2, 6, 29, 37, 43.

[11]Jeremiah 51:64.

[12]Evelyn Klingel-Brandt, "Babylon," *The Oxford Encyclopedia of Archaeology in the Near East*, vol. 1 (New York: Oxford University Press, 1997), p. 255.

[13]Jeremiah 51:37.

[14]Jeremiah 51:43.

[15]Iraq Tourism Board (http://www.uruklink.net/tourism/eindex1.htm; retrieved May 30, 2002).

[16]Daniel 4:30.

[17]Klingel-Brandt, "Babylon."

[18]Klingel-Brandt, "Babylon."

[19]Genesis 11:4.

[20]Klingel-Brandt, "Babylon."

[21]Charles Dyer with Angela Elwell Hunt, *The Rise of Babylon: Sign of the End Times* (Wheaton: Tyndale House, 1991), p. 27.

[22]"Saddam Hussein and Babylon: Prelude to Armageddon?" Hope of Israel (http://hope-of-israel.org/saddam.htm; retrieved June 4, 2002).

[23]Revelation 17:10.

[24]Revelation 17:18. It is possible that not the Antichrist but a preceding European leader, mentioned in Revelation 17:10, will rule from Babylon.

[25]Revelation 17:16; Revelation 18.

[26]Revelation 17:17.

WHO IS JESUS CHRIST?

═══════════════════════════════

In the final analysis, the conflict that threatens our world is rooted in deeply held religious beliefs. Religious Jews believe their Bible proves that God gave them the land they currently occupy. Palestinian Muslims twist the teachings of the Old Testament and claim the promises were actually made to *their* ancestors. But a far greater issue than land divides these three major world religions. Proponents of Judaism, Islam and Christianity do not agree on the person and work of Jesus Christ. While many Jews are awaiting their Messiah, most refuse to believe it is Jesus Christ. Muslims believe that Jesus Christ is coming again, but consider Him to be merely a prophet. Christianity has always maintained that Jesus Christ is God who became man. Many Christians also believe that Jesus Christ will return just as He promised and will actually rule over the entire earth from the city of Jerusalem for a thousand years.

WHICH JESUS?

Consider this account of the "final days." Crowds of followers clamor for his attention as he travels the entire world, performing miracles and appearing to raise people from the dead. He claims to be a prophet. In fact, he claims to be God himself — and the masses do not protest. He rewards the men and women who follow him. He starves those who do not.[1]

Then Jesus returns to deal with this deceiver.

He descends from heaven and personally battles this man, the Antichrist, killing him. Jesus ushers in a period of unparalleled calm, justice, and prosperity, governing all the nations on earth as a righteous ruler and judge. Peace, harmony, and tranquility prevail while false religions die.

Illness ceases. Poisonous animals lose their venom. Wild beasts suddenly become gentle creatures. If a small child places his hand in a snake's mouth, he is not harmed. If a little girl playfully opens a lion's mouth, she is safe. Cattle graze with cheetahs, camels with lions, goats with jackals.

People no longer give to the poor; there are no poor! Agricultural fertility increases incredibly; seeds planted on solid rock sprout. Milk flows freely; a single cow provides milk for an entire tribe.[2]

Reading this scenario, most of us would assume it comes from the Bible. In reality, it comes from the teachings of Muhammad, the founder of Islam, who was born around 570 AD. Yet every portion of this account faintly echoes the Bible. The Muslim Scriptures borrow many of their "end times" beliefs from the teachings of God's Word, the Bible. Thus, many Muslims survey today's world, and much like their Bible-believing neighbors, they see the "end" approaching. But for Muslims, the key characters and the final outcome are contrary to what the Bible clearly teaches.

THE BIBLE OR THE KORAN?

In fact, the Jesus described in the Muslim Scriptures is not the same Jesus we find in the Bible. One of the most striking differences between the two teachings about Jesus surfaces in the accounts of Jesus' relationship with the Antichrist. The Bible teaches that the Antichrist will persecute the Jews for three-and-a-half years, aiming to erase them from civilization. Then Jesus will save His people, the Jews, from this power-crazed leader. Islam, on the other hand, declares the Jews are the *allies* of the Antichrist! Many Muslims follow a doctrine that teaches Jesus will lead His followers in *slaughtering* the Jews.

So those of us who trust in the Jesus of the Bible should not expect any friendly feelings from those who believe in a Jesus devoted to killing Jews. Nor should we expect Islamic terrorism to gradually fade away. It is not a fad. Many aspects of Muslim extremism are firmly rooted in time-honored Muslim teachings.

So which Jesus *will* return to earth? Will it be the

Jesus of Christianity, who comes to deliver the Jews? Or will it be a vastly different Jesus, the Jesus of Islam, who comes to destroy the Jews? If our heart's desire is to follow Jesus, and if we truly want to know who Jesus is, we must choose between the Jesus of the Bible and the Jesus of the Koran.[3]

At first glance, the Jesus of the Bible and the Jesus of Muhammad appear similar. The Koran and other Muslim holy books refer to Jesus often, with teachings that frequently parallel the Bible's account. The Bible teaches that Jesus did not come to earth in the normal way, but was born of a virgin. Muslims agree. The Bible proclaims Jesus the Messiah, the Word of God, a prophet sent by God. Muslims agree. Muslims also teach that Jesus was a perfect man who could perceive others' secrets. And they believe that Jesus' message is substantiated by miracles — including raising the dead.[4]

Clearly, both Muslims and Christians respect Jesus as a great prophet. Since this is the truth, why must we still choose between the Jesus of the Bible and the Jesus of Muhammad? On the surface there might seem to be similarities, but in reality, Muhammad denies many of the Bible's teachings about Jesus . . . teachings that tell us who Jesus really is. The Bible teaches that Jesus is the Son of God in human flesh. The Koran denies this. The Bible declares Jesus the Redeemer of the world, the One who died in our place on the cross. The Koran denies redemption for man, teaching that we can earn heaven through our own good behavior. So it is not surprising that the Koran also concludes that

Jesus *didn't die on the cross*. Why would we need a Savior to die on the cross for us if we were capable of earning heaven by our own works? Muslims teach that God took Jesus directly to heaven rather than letting Him die.

Page after page of the Koran contains Bible personalities and terminology. However, Islam rejects the very core of the Christian faith. Thus, Islam is a religion vastly different from Christianity.

In their early days of training, anthropologists must learn to distinguish between what people *say* they do and what they *actually* do. Anthropologists who have forgotten this lesson have written some very amusing reports. For example, Dr. Margaret Mead, in *Coming of Age in Samoa*, portrayed a free-love paradise in which young people had promiscuous relations with abandon and without guilt. According to Dr. Mead, this was a paradise in which rape did not exist. How could rape occur, when youngsters were engaging in sex as casually as one would shake another's hand? Mead learned all about this paradise, of course, from her teenage informants. She did not consider the possibility that some of the stories she heard might be fabricated — telling her what she wanted to hear. The thought never entered her mind to wander over to the courthouses of Samoa, where dozens of rape cases filled the dockets.

In fact, there is no paradise on this earth. Everywhere in the world, *we all fall short* of our own standards of righteousness. We are not what we ought to be. Every religion tries to explain and alleviate this problem of human sin. Some religions regard sin as an illusion, just a big mistake, an example of very poor judgment. Since sin abounds in everyday life, such religions usually conclude that everyday life is nothing more than an illusion. Some of these religions proceed to tell us that the world we see around us doesn't really exist.

The Christian solution for the problem of sin is vastly different. We are all sinners. The Bible tells us we all deserve punishment. But God has sent Jesus Christ to *rescue* us. When Jesus was nailed to the cross, He suffered the punishment we deserve — He paid the price for our wrongdoing. He took our place and died for our sins. Then, after three days, Jesus rose from the dead in victory over death and sin. Our sin is real, not an illusion . . . and it is serious. It deserves punishment. Escape from that punishment occurs immediately when an individual accepts Jesus Christ as Savior. This must be a personal choice or decision.

Christianity enables flawed men and women to face the evil within them without flinching. Christians have the freedom to admit who they really are before God — no matter how vile and ugly their lives have been. Christians also freely acknowledge complete reliance upon Jesus and His death on the cross — as the only way of salvation. This salvation is a gift to be received by faith. We could never earn it.[5]

ISLAM HAS NO USE FOR THE CROSS

Islam provides a completely different answer to the problem of sin. Islam naturally leads its followers to *project* evil onto the outsiders, the non-Muslims. *They're* the bad ones. "*We*, the Muslims, are the good ones," they say, "We are good enough to get into paradise through our own efforts." This type of thinking can be found in Christendom, of course. But it is clearly a completely non-Christian idea, because it minimizes the worth of the death of Jesus Christ on the cross.

But an us-versus-them way of thinking is *rightfully* part of Islam. It lies at the very core of the religion itself. At the last judgment, the Koran teaches, humans will be placed on a scale. Those whose good deeds weigh enough will go to paradise. The others will go to hell. Muslims will go to heaven and others will go to hell, because the Muslims are "good people" and the others are "bad people."[6]

How vastly different this is from the Christian teaching that we are *all* wrongdoers. We are *all* in the same boat! Muslims are in reality sinners, just like the rest of us, but their religious beliefs prompt them to deny the truth. Their Islamic world-view encourages them to pass through life wearing blinders that prevent them from frankly confronting their own sins.

At the same time, however, Islam allows them 20/20 vision for non-Muslims' transgressions. Islam teaches men and women to love their neighbors who are like them — in other words, their neighbors who are Muslim. The Koran teaches Muslims to hate even their own people, if they are not Muslim. "There is for you an excellent example in Abraham and those with him, when they said to their people,

'We are clear of you and of whatever ye worship besides Allah: we have rejected you, and there has arisen, between us and you, enmity and hatred for ever, unless ye believe in Allah and Him alone.'"[7] The Bible does not record any such statement by the Old Testament saint Abraham or his companions. On the contrary, the Jesus of the Bible teaches men and women to love *all* their neighbors, even their enemies, because we are all alike.

Everything we know about the "Jesus" of Islam ultimately comes from the testimony of Muhammad, the founder of Islam. Islam's principal book, the Koran, was delivered to Muhammad alone. All Muslim spiritual traditions originate with him. In order to consider which Jesus is worthy of our respect, which Jesus is real, we need to look at Muhammad's teachings, his life, and his claims of divine inspiration.

THE TEACHINGS OF JESUS AND OF MUHAMMAD

In light of the Koran's many teachings about Jesus, it is puzzling how much Muhammad's teachings contrast with those of Jesus as recorded in the Bible. As we have seen, Muhammad taught that Jesus never died on the cross. He claims that people just *thought* they had seen him die. Yet according to the Bible, Jesus Himself told His disciples no less than ten times during the week in which He was nailed to a cross that he would be crucified and would then rise again within three days. Muslims often say the Bible cannot be trusted, claiming Christians and Jews changed it and have corrupted it through the years. Yet many details of Jesus' death and resurrection are predicted in Old Testament prophecies. Today we can still read those prophecies in scrolls that were transcribed *before Jesus was ever born*. If these ancient prophecies were corrupted, then how were the biblical prophets able to predict exactly when Jesus would come, where he would be born, and a myriad of other details about His life? The prophecies, written long before Jesus was born, also described how the coming Messiah would die for our sins on a cross.[8]

Again, Jesus taught His followers to love their enemies. Muhammad taught his followers to hate and kill their enemies. In fact, he ordered them to kill *all* idol-worshipers, whether they were enemies or not![9]

Jesus taught that the Old Testament Bible of His day was the very Word of God. He quoted from the Bible frequently and accurately. He regarded everything in the Bible as truth. Since World War II, we have unearthed very ancient copies of the Old Testament, some from before Jesus' time. Now we can see with our own eyes that Jesus' Bible is the same Old Testament that Christians and Jews possess today. Yet Muhammad's teachings contradict the Bible at *hundreds* of points. Muhammad teaches that when the great Flood came, one of Noah's sons refused to enter the ark and drowned. The Bible, of course, tells us that all three of Noah's sons, along with their wives (each had only one wife), entered the ark, and repopulated the earth after the flood. These variations are typical. Muhammad's revelations frequently sound like the garbled accounts of an imaginative storyteller who has heard the Bible's accounts not secondhand, but third or fourth hand. Should we then heed Muhammad's "Jesus" or the Jesus of the Bible?

THE LIVES OF JESUS AND OF MUHAMMAD

Muhammad lived from around 570 AD to 632 AD. He assumes a role in Islam vastly different from the role of Jesus in Christianity. Muslims do not worship Muhammad or look to him for their salvation (they expect to be saved by their own good works). But both religions are very devoted to their founders and look to them as supreme role models. This pride and admiration is understandable. Yet Jesus and Muhammad were very different men. The more respect one has for Muhammad, the less reason there is to reverence Jesus. The opposite is true as well. While respecting the loyalties of both Muslims and Christians, we must choose between Muhammad and the Jesus of the Bible. We cannot follow and serve both. Perhaps the contrast between the two men is most clearly seen in their attitudes toward religious enemies, unbelievers, and women in general.

Muslims admire Muhammad as a great warrior. In fact, many historians consider Muhammad one of history's greatest generals. Rising from obscurity, be built up a military force that gained remarkable victories over armies much larger than his own. In less than a century, Muslim armies conquered a vast portion of the world. In fact, warfare quickly became the prime missionary tool of the Muslims. It should be noted that no nation has ever initially turned to Islam except "by the sword."

Jesus, on the other hand, refused to bear arms in defense of His religion — or even to save His own life. Instead, He died for all mankind. That includes those who crucified Him. He prayed, "Father, forgive them, for they do not know what they are doing."

Muslims admire Muhammad's ability to stand up for his beliefs. According to Muslim historians, Muhammad repeatedly urged his followers to kill people who disagreed with him. For instance, one woman was put to death because she composed a poem that compared Muhammad unfavorably with Tubba, a ruler from Yemen. A man over one hundred years old was executed for disagreeing with Muhammad! Muhammad also ordered his followers to kill slaves and pregnant women.[10]

Like Muhammad, Jesus was resolute in the face of opposition. Jesus claimed the power to call a legion of angels for assistance against His enemies. But instead Jesus chose to die on behalf of mankind — including His enemies. When one of His disciples (Peter) attempted to defend Jesus with a sword, Jesus rebuked him. Muhammad promoted violence to suppress opposition. Jesus conquered, not with violence, but with love.

Muslims admire Muhammad for his manliness.

The Koran allows men up to four wives. Muhammad claimed God made an exception for him so he could have more than four wives. Jesus, on the other hand, remained single in order to devote his life to others.

Christians admire Jesus, not only as their Savior, but as their example, as well. Muslims, too, find much to admire in the founder of their religion. But the two men are such opposites that it is difficult to imagine anyone giving allegiance to both of them.

WHO SPEAKS FOR GOD?

Jesus claimed to be God's spokesman. This claim was confirmed by Old Testament prophecies, by His virgin birth, and by the miracles He performed. He was declared to be the Son of God by His resurrection from the dead. Christ's ascension into heaven, after His resurrection, also confirms the deity of Jesus. Muslims and Christians alike have solid reasons to follow the Jesus of the Bible.

Muhammad's claim to be God's prophet, on the other hand, is substantiated only by his own say-so. That's it. The Koran tells us that Muhammad is God's prophet, but the Koran was revealed to Muhammad — and no one else! If we accept Muhammad's Jesus, we accept Him on the strength of Muhammad's own word — the strength of Muhammad's own character.

A gap wider than the Grand Canyon of Arizona lies between the Jesus of the Bible and Muhammad and his "Jesus." We have to decide. Do we want to follow the example of Muhammad, a man who was supremely effective in *killing* his enemies? Or do we want to be loyal to the One who was supremely effective in *saving* His enemies? Do we want to follow a man who built his religion by destroying unbelievers? Above all, do we believe that we need a Redeemer in order to face a Holy God? Or, are we convinced that we can be good enough on our own?

A FINAL QUESTION

The holy books of Muslims and the Christian Bible tell us that Jesus is the Word of God. He was miraculously born of a virgin; Muhammad was not. The Bible records many of Jesus' miracles . . . miracles that proved He came from God. The Koran reports *no* miracles performed by Muhammad. The Bible and the Koran both tell us to follow Jesus. Why should we want to follow anyone else?

But following Jesus involves more than just regarding Him as a great man. It means following Him to the cross and accepting what He accomplished there for us. The Bible tells us we are all sinners . . . we have done wrong. And God cannot accept sin. It is contrary to His very nature. This means that we all deserve to be separated from God forever. In eternity, when this world's props and diversions are left behind, separation from God will result in eternal anguish.

But God sent Jesus, His Son, to earth because His desire is that none of us experience eternal death. God's Son has always existed — He *is* God. But when He came into the world as Jesus Christ, He became a man, without giving up His Godhood. This is a point of great significance. Jesus is not just another prophet . . . He is the unique God-man. He is able to identify with you and with me. He can be our representative before God. So Jesus came to the earth as a baby, grew up, lived a perfect life, and finally offered Himself to suffer death *in our place*. He didn't have to die for his own wrongdoing, but He was willing to die for yours and mine. And He did. He was nailed to a cross, died, and was buried. Then, on the third day after His death, Jesus rose from the dead. God the Father accepted His sacrifice on the cross, and Jesus returned to life in victory over sin and death. We cannot make ourselves good enough for God. But Jesus is already good enough, and he has paid the penalty that we have coming. Since He has already suffered our death penalty for us, the Bible proclaims, we don't have to do *anything* to gain God's favor. Jesus has already purchased salvation for us. We only have to trust in Him as our Savior, as the One who died for our sins. Then we immediately become God's children, says the Bible. Instead of eternal *death*, we possess eternal *life*. As the Bible's best-known verse says it, "God loved the world so much that He gave His only Son, so that whoever trusts in Him will not die, but will have eternal life."[11]

If you have not yet trusted in Jesus as your Savior, I urge you to do that right now. There are no special words you have to say. All that God asks is that you trust in His Son, Jesus Christ, as the One who died for you. But you may want to repeat God's own words back to Him, applying them to yourself. You might say something like this: "God, you loved the world so much that You gave Your only Son, so that whoever trusts in Him will not die, but will have eternal life. I, _____ (your name) trust in you, Jesus Christ, as my Savior. Please forgive my sins and give me the gift of eternal life. Thank you for dying on the cross for me. Amen."

Once you come to know Jesus Christ personally, you will look at the world differently. As you study the Bible, your mind is renewed with truth. You will soon discover that the Christian life is allowing Jesus to live His life through you. You begin to respond to others the way that He would respond; and you begin to love others the way that He loves.

Through prayer, worship and Bible study you will draw closer and closer to Jesus and you will naturally look forward to His coming. Might He return soon? As the 9/11 Generation, we have every reason to be filled with expectation and hope!

Chapter Eleven Endnotes

[1]Muhammad Ali Ibn Zubair Ali, "Who is the evil Dajjal (the "anti-Christ")?" (http://www.islam.tc/prophecies/masdaj.html; retrieved June 3, 2002).

[2]A. H. Elias, "Jesus (Isa) A.S. in Islam, and his Second Coming" (http://www.islam.tc/prophecies/jesus.html; retrieved June 3, 2002).

[3]There are many other differences between the role of Jesus in Muslim and biblical accounts of the end times. For example, Muslims teach that after his return to earth Jesus will marry, have children, and then die and be buried. Most significantly, Jesus is not the most important end-times figure in Muslim teaching. Rather, a different man, the Mahdi — "The guided one" — will be Allah's personal representative in the end times. See A.H. Elias and Mohammad Ali ibn Zubair Ali,

"Imam Mahdi (Descendent of Prophet Muhammad PBUH)," (http://www.islam.tc/prophecies/imam.html; retrieved June 3, 2002).

[4]"The Distinctives of the Lord Jesus-Christ in the Koran," thegrace.com (http://www.thegrace.com/about.html; retrieved June 3, 2002).

[5]Ephesians 2:8, 9.

[6]Norman L. Geisler and Abdul Saleeb, *Answering Islam* (Grand Rapids: Baker Book House, 1993), p. 117.

[7]Koran, Sura 60:4. On the Koran's attitude toward those who do not accept Islam, see Sura 3:118: "O ye who believe! Take not into your intimacy those outside your ranks: They will not fail to corrupt you. They only desire your ruin: Rank hatred has already appeared from their mouths: What their hearts conceal is far worse. We have made plain to you the Signs, if ye have wisdom."

[8]For example, Psalm 22 describes the death of Jesus in detail. Verses 16 through 18 describe the moment of crucifixion: "Dogs have surrounded me; a band of evil men has encircled me, they have pierced my hadns and my feet. I can count all my bones; people stare and gloat over me. They divide my garments among them and cast lots for my clothing."

[9]Koran, Sura 9:5.

[10]"Muhammad, Islam, and Terrorism," *Answering Islam* (http://answering-islam.org/Silas/terrorism.htm#plea; retrieved June 3, 2002).

[11]John 3:16.

AFTERWORD

W e *should* have seen it coming. September 11's slice of Armageddon followed years of warnings. Osama bin Laden and other Muslim extremists made it clear they intended to act out their apocalyptic fantasies of conquest and annihilation. The signs were there; we just weren't paying attention. Here are just a few of the thousands of terrorist acts that in retrospect read like dress rehearsals for September 11:

- **December 29, 1992:** In what U.S. intelligence agencies believe was the first terrorist attack involving Osama bin Laden, a bomb explodes in a hotel in Aden, Yemen, where U.S. troops have been staying. The blast kills two Austrian tourists. Two Islamic militants trained in Afghanistan are arrested.
- **February 26, 1993:** A van packed with explosives detonates in a parking garage below the World Trade Center in New York, killing six people and wounding more than one thousand.

The mastermind of the bombing, Ramzi Yousef, is believed to be financially linked to Osama bin Laden.

- **January, 1995:** The CIA and FBI learn of "Project Bojinka," a plan by terrorists with ties to Osama bin Laden to hijack commercial airplanes and fly them into targets such as CIA headquarters in Langley, Virginia.

- **November 13, 1995:** A car bomb explodes at the U.S. military headquarters in Riyadh, Saudi Arabia, killing seven people, five of them Americans. In their confession, the four terrorists accused of the crime claim to have read communiqués from Osama bin Laden.

- **June 25, 1996:** A truck bomb outside the Khobar Towers in Dharan, Saudi Arabia, kills nineteen American servicemen. U.S. investigators believe Osama bin Laden is linked to the attack.

- **September 5, 1996**: Ramzi Yousef, Abdul Murad, and Wali Khan Amin Shah are convicted in a New York federal court for their part in Project Bojinka, the plan by Muslim terrorists with links to Osama bin Laden to hijack commercial airplanes and fly them into American targets.

- **February 23, 1998:** Osama bin Laden and his associates issue a fatwa, a Muslim religious ruling, stating, "We—with Allah's help—call on every Muslim who believes in Allah and wishes to be rewarded to comply with Allah's order to kill the Americans and plunder their money wherever and whenever they find it."

- **August 7, 1998:** Car bombs explode outside the U.S. embassies in Nairobi, Kenya, and Dar es Salaam, Tanzania, killing 224 people. Osama bin Laden is believed to be behind the attacks.
- **September 15, 1999:** The US National Commission on National Security/21st Century (Hart-Rudman) warns that in the next quarter-century "States, terrorists, and other disaffected groups will acquire weapons of mass destruction and mass disruption, and some will use them. Americans will likely die on American soil, possibly in large numbers."[1]
- **April 15, 2000:** The Hart-Rudman Commision warns, "Americans are less secure than they believe themselves to be. The time for reexamination is now, before the American people find themselves shocked by events they never anticipated."[2]
- **October 12, 2000:** The US Navy ship USS Cole is bombed while docked in Yemen's port of Aden. Seventeen sailors on board are killed. Osama bin Laden appears to have planned this attack.
- **February 15, 2001:** The Hart-Rudman Commission recommends specific changes in the US security system to address the danger of "mass-casualty terrorism directed against the US homeland . . ."[3]
- **August 17, 2001:** The FBI arrests Zacarias Moussaoui, an Algerian who applied to a flight

school to learn how to steer a Boeing 747 aircraft. He had no interest in takeoffs or landings. Moussaoui has been linked to Osama bin Laden.[4]

WHAT WENT WRONG?

We should have seen September 11 coming. Multiplied warning signs pointed toward the coming attacks, but for the most part we ignored them. No wonder *Terrorism and Security Monitor*'s special edition on the September 11, 2001 attacks refers to "September 11: Anatomy of an Intelligence Failure."[5] Why did our nation neglect to take decisive action in the face of so many warning signals?

Deadly Distractions

On September 10, 2001, Americans had more pressing issues to worry about than the remote possibility that a group of fanatics would successfully attack New York City, the world's financial capital. If our thoughts turned to foreign affairs, many of us would simply breathe a sigh of relief – the Cold War has ended. For the first time in our lives, the looming threat of global war and annihilation seemed to have passed. With urgent action-items clamoring for our attention, most of us focused on the immediate, the here and now, giving little thought for any future danger. In other words, we were distracted.

The American intelligence community, too, was distracted in the years leading up to September 11.

The Clinton administration's numerous military engagements taxed the resources of understaffed intelligence agencies, resulting in such blunders as the bombing of the Chinese embassy in Belgrade in May of 1999. President Clinton himself, meanwhile, was preoccupied by issues far removed from the growing terrorist threat. When associates of Osama bin Laden exploded a lethal bomb in the World Trade Center in 1993, President Clinton did not visit the site of the attack. Issues such as economic recession and the treatment of homosexuals in the military loomed larger on the agenda of the new President, who had been in office for less than two months. Two years later, the nation of Sudan offered to turn Osama bin Laden over to the United States for prosecution. The U.S., with its attention focused elsewhere, turned down the offer.[6]

Later in his Presidency, Mr. Clinton devoted most of his energy to simply staying in office. He was more concerned about personal scandal than he was about global terrorism. As former Clinton political consultant Dick Morris puts it, "Blame whoever you want, but we were without a president from January, 1998 until April, 1999." Morris is convinced that Clinton's failure to mobilize America to confront foreign terror in the years following the 1993 attack led directly to the disaster on September 11.[7]

It is easy to allow immediate demands to distract us from other critical concerns. When the urgent overshadows the important, it is merely a matter of time before a price is paid.

A Warning Ignored

It is not surprising that the US largely ignored pointed warnings like those issued by the Hart-Rudman commission, stressing the need for a national defense stance appropriate to the twenty-first century. This commission enjoyed the support of both the Democratic President and the Republican-controlled Congress. It received support—but it did not receive a great deal of attention. Their conclusion was actually a prediction, "Americans will likely die on American soil, possibly in large numbers."[8]

This response, or rather lack of response, is scarcely surprising. After all, government warnings have become so frequent that for many of us they seem almost routine. Warning fatigue, some observers have called it. When we hear repeated alarms and yet disaster doesn't arrive, we may begin to tune out the too-familiar cry of "Wolf!"

Until there comes the time when there really *is* a wolf.

Before 911 the inclination was to ignore or discount the numerous warnings received at the State Department and other government agencies. January 7,1999, Hisham Kabbani, founder of the Islamic Supreme Council for America, spoke at a State Department event and stated that bin Laden's organization was able to buy atomic weapons from the Russian Mafia, using opium as currency. Despite his incredible courage, Kabbani's words were largely ignored.

A False Security

In one sense, September 11 is familiar territory to Americans. For decades now, post-apocalyptic movies have regaled us with visions of our great cities in ruins. In Tom Clancy's 1994 best-selling novel *Debt of Honor*, a hate-filled foreign pilot slams a commercial airliner into the Capitol while the President is addressing a joint session of Congress; most of the nation's leaders are wiped out. Many men and women have become wealthy by entertaining us with such images of our own destruction.

But we never intended these images to jump from the screen into our lives. The thought of viewing such devastation, not in a fictional fantasy, but in our streets, was too staggering to imagine. Who could picture a couple of jumbo jets actually slamming into two of the tallest structures in New York, one of them nearly breaking into pieces as it accelerated toward the speed of sound? Who could seriously think that talented young men would spend years in this country, unobtrusively working, studying—all the time waiting, waiting for the signal that would give them the chance to kill thousands of ordinary Americans? Who could believe that intelligent, disciplined people would actually sacrifice their lives in the service of Osama bin Laden's farrago of transparent lies? Such actions may seem plausible in the made-up landscapes of novels and movies. But in real life? Things like that don't actually happen — not in America!

Not until now.

A WAKE-UP CALL FROM HELL?

The destruction of the World Trade Center in September 2001 was the bloodiest foreign attack on US soil and the most devastating terrorist operation in history. It is inevitable that we should speak of it in apocalyptic terms. To describe the event's enormity, our minds naturally turn to the tragic poetry of the biblical prophets. We look to words like those of the prophet Joel referring to "a day of darkness and gloom, a day of clouds and blackness . . . Before them fire devours, behind them a flame blazes. Before them the land is like the Garden of Eden, behind them a desert waste—nothing escapes them."[9] The parallel between Osama bin Laden's evil scheme and the devastation catalogued in the prophetic books of the Bible is stark.

Yet, as terrible as the destruction of the World Trade Center was, the Bible tells us that even greater disasters are in store. For all its horror, September 11 was only a preview of things to come, a scale model of the apocalypse. The Bible warns us that global plagues lie ahead on a scale we can barely imagine — unheard-of levels of famine, war, disease, and destruction that come raining down from the sky. Muslim terrorists may have given us a taste of what is to come, a sort of hellish hors d'ouevres, but it is only a taste. Finally, says God's Word, this entire world will perish — and those who place their hopes and trust in this world will perish with it.

But we have never seen any of these plagues. Might they not be thousands of years in the future?

Are they really coming at all? Questions like these are not surprising. We can expect to hear them on the lips of Americans today—a nation of people distracted, weary of sky-is-falling rhetoric, and understandably reluctant to think about disasters so massive that they cut off great slices of the world's population in a space of a few seconds. But if our nation now regrets its willingness to ignore the clues preceding the September 11 outrage, Christians should think twice before pushing aside evidence that the climax of history itself may be drawing near. And, as we have seen throughout this book, there *is* such evidence, in a substantial and steadily mounting body. Even secularists are openly pondering the fate of the planet. In the past few decades, through times of war and peace, through periods of prosperity and depression, the world stage has steadily been refashioned into a fitting backdrop for the end-time drama described by the ancient prophets. Today, as never before, we can see prophetic events casting their shadows before them.

Consider again just some of the indications that the world of the Apocalypse is imminent:

- **August 6, 1945:** The "Little Boy" atomic bomb is dropped on Hiroshima, beginning the atomic age, in which apocalyptic mass destruction suddenly becomes easily conceivable.
- **May 14, 1948:** Nearly 2,000 years after its destruction, Israel is miraculously reborn as a nation, set to assume the prominent role the

Bible assigns it in end-time events.

- **August 22, 1948:** The World Council of Churches, a fellowship of churches "from virtually all christian [sic] traditions,"[10] is founded, paving the way for later ecumenical efforts and the end-time global religious system described by the biblical prophets.
- **March 25, 1957:** The Treaty of Rome formally establishes the European Economic Community in order to "lay the foundations of an ever closer union among the peoples of Europe" reminiscent of the ancient Roman Empire. The Bible predicts a resurgent Roman Empire in the last days.[11]
- **June 5, 1967:** In the Six Day War, Jerusalem returns to Jewish control for the first time since antiquity. The nation that is to rebuild the temple in the last days once again rules the city in which that temple is to be rebuilt.
- **July 10, 1962:** The Telstar communications satellite inaugurates an era of instantaneous global communication, removing from the realm of science fiction the Bible's claim that in the final days people across the globe will observe events in Jerusalem as they occur.
- **March 26, 1975:** The Biological Weapons Convention, the first international treaty to ban an entire class of weapons, goes into force. Recognizing the overwhelming destructive potential of their own weaponry, earth's nations attempt to fend off the apocalypse.
- **September 1987:** Iraqi dictator Saddam

Hussein hosts the First International Babylon Festival, celebrating the progress of his project to restore the ancient glories of the city.[12] The Bible identifies "Babylon the Great" as a major end-times governmental and commercial center that is ultimately to be destroyed in a single hour.[13]

- **September 13, 1993:** In the Oslo Accords, Israel grants self-government to the Palestinians and the PLO recognizes Israel's right to exist.[14] The treaty's five-year phased implementation may serve as a model for the seven-year treaty that is to launch what the Bible calls a time of tribulation.

- **December 1999:** Turkey, a prominent part of the Roman Empire that is located in Asia, not Europe, is admitted as a candidate for full membership in the *European* Economic Community, moving the borders of the union closer those of ancient Rome.

- **July 29, 2001:** The Temple Mount Faithful, an Israeli group dedicated to rebuilding the Jerusalem temple, attempts to lay the cornerstone for the new temple, sparking violent Muslim rioting. Israeli police prevent the Faithful from reaching the Temple Mount.[15]

- **January 1, 2002:** As the European Economic Community increasingly assumes the role of the unified Roman Empire prophesied in Scripture, the national currencies of most member nations are replaced by a central European currency, the Euro.

How can we ignore events like these...events that are bringing the world ever closer to the Bible's end-times scenario? Should we decide that the convergence of seemingly unrelated incidents into a clear biblical pattern is purely coincidental? The pace of fulfillment is intensifying. Should we ignore that trend, too? Some of these occurrences, such as the rebirth of Israel and today's obsessive push for peace in the Middle East, fit the biblical picture so closely that the effect is eerie, even for nonbelievers. Yet many Christians have overlooked these historical developments completely, as though the biblical prophecies had never been written. Why?

MORE AND MORE SIGNS

Just as we had other things on our minds as the previews of September 11 accumulated, so today the pressure of overloaded schedules and a hectic lifestyle prevents many of us from exploring the wisdom and discovering the encouragement found in biblical prophecy. Many Americans, too, have been put off by past encounters with the predictions of self-appointed prophets. And the events prophesied in the Bible may have seemed too big — too cataclysmic — for us to take in, or even to think about.

Time to Focus

One of the most striking characteristics of American Christians during the past fifty years is how similar we have become to our non-believing friends. This is not all bad — after all, the US is not "the great Satan" that Muslim radicals paint us to be. But there are serious cracks in the structure of American culture, and they affect the nation's believers along with everyone else. For example, surveys indicate that in America the tragedy of divorce strikes churchgoers as frequently as it does the rest of the population.[16] And, like our neighbors, many of us focus our attention exclusively on the here and now. We devote our lives to the pursuit of attractive homes, expensive toys, and financial security. We are distracted — too distracted to let the Bible set our personal agenda. Too distracted to hear the Bible's insistent reminder that this world is not our home. Too distracted to listen to the prophets as they tell us, again and again, that soon this world will not be *anyone's* home.

Balance, NOT Cynicism

Many American believers have been burned by misguided and self-promoting "experts" who have specified dates for the rapture, the prophetic moment when the Lord will come for His followers, suddenly removing them from the earth to join Him forever. Cultists have long lured people into their ranks with such promises, but now some evangelicals, too, have taken to specifying dates for the rapture. For example, Edgar C. Whisenant, a retired NASA engineer, wrote in his book *88 Reasons Why the Rapture Could be in 1988* that this biblical rapture would occur between September 11 and September 13,

1988. Over 4.5 million of his books were printed. When those dates passed without incident, Christians who had been taken in by his reasoning were profoundly disillusioned. Some of them decided not to concern themselves with prophecy any more. In the following decade, Harold Camping, a prominent Christian radio personality, authored *1994?* and *Are You Ready?,* predicting the rapture on September 6, 1994. Again, Christians were disappointed and skeptics had a field day.

Those who know the Bible best realize that the date-setters cannot be right. The Bible clearly tells us the Lord may come for His own at *any* time; it urges us to plan and look for this exhilarating moment *all* the time. We cannot allow those who have mishandled biblical truth to blind us to the incredible events unfolding in our world, pointing us to the culmination of God's plan for the earth.

The Unthinkable Will Be Reality

Many of the events portrayed in biblical prophecy are difficult to imagine. When the Bible describes locusts with human faces attacking millions of people across the globe or a star that falls to the earth and pollutes one third of its waters, to many Americans this sounds more like science fiction— *early* science fiction—than anything else. It is difficult to wrap our minds around many of the biblical images. It is also difficult to come to terms with the immense scale of devastation predicted in the Bible. Repeatedly, we are told, plagues and disasters will

wipe away a major proportion of the earth's population. In fact, Jesus told his disciples that God has
decided to shorten the coming tribulation. Otherwise, there would be *no* survivors! It is easy for
many believers simply to skip over such extreme,
even outlandish-sounding, portions of the Bible.

Yet the unnerving fact remains — we can see the
world careening toward the apocalypse. Each day,
so-called "normal life" takes on more of the col-
oration of the Bible's "outlandish" end times era.
The world is poised for the end of history. It *can*
happen here.

The events put into motion by 9/11 fit the Bible's
picture of the end times — fit it hand-in-glove.
There's no need to wait for the movie — the world
we live in today *is* the movie version of the Bible's
end-time prophecies.

Afterword Endnotes

[1]Gary Hart, Warren Rudman, *et al.,Seeking a National Strategy: A
Concert for Preserving Security and Promoting Freedom*, p. 5
(http://www.nssg.gov/PhaseII.pdf).

[2]Gary Hart, Warren Rudman, *et al., New World Coming: American
Security in the 21st Century* (http://www.fas.org/man/docs/nwc/
nwc.htm).

[3]Gary Hart, Warren Rudman, *et al., New World Coming: American
Security in the 21st Century* (http://www.fas.org/man/docs/nwc/
nwc.htm).

[4]Julian Borger, Vikram Dodd, and Paul Kelso, "Shoe Bomb Linked to
bin Laden," *The Guardian*, December 29, 2001 (http://www.
guardian.co.uk/september11/story/0,11209,625563,00.html)

[5]http://www.janes.com/security/international_security/news/jtsm/jts
m_promo_011019.shtml

[6] Dick Morris "Clinton's Failure to Mobilize America to Confront Foreign Terror after the 1993 Attack Led Directly to 9-11 Disaster," *Jewish World Review*, November 14, 2001.

[7] Dick Morris "Clinton's Failure," *Jewish World Review*, November 14, 2001.

[8] Gary Hart, Warren Rudman, *et al., New World Coming: American Security in the 21st Century* (http://www.fas.org/man/docs/nwc/nwc. htm).

[9] Joel 2:2-3.

[10] World Council of Churches home page, http://www.wcc-coe.org/wcc/english.html.

[11] http://www.cerebalaw.com/rome.htm; http://members.tripod.com/crass69/1957.html.

[12] The festival's official theme was "From Nebuchadnezzar to Saddam Hussein, Babylon undergoes a renaissance." (http://www.ortzion.org/calndr_end3.html).

"The restoration of Babylon began in 1978 to save what remained of the city from the destructive effects of local salt deposits, a high water table and pillaging from local villagers. In part because most young Iraqi men were away at the war with Iran, and in part because native laborers often lacked the required skills, Babylon has largely been rebuilt through the hands of over eighteen hundred Egyptian, Sudanese, Chinese and South Korean laborers.

"The Iraqis are determined that the new Babylon will look as nearly like the old as possible. No one is exactly sure how the ancient city looked. Scholars, however, are studying archaeological data and other information from ancient Sumerian and Babylonian writings in order to make sure that the restored Babylon is authentic."

—Charles H. Dyer, The Rise of Babylon, cited at http://goldenminutes.org/Bible%20Study/Worlds%20in%20Collision/Lesson%207. htm

Hussein evidently plans to rebuild the entire city. The Web site http://www.zionministry.com/babylon.html reports that the following inscription is found among the ancient city's reconstructed buildings: "In the era of President Saddam Hussein all Babylon was constructed in three stages. From Nebuchadnezzar to Saddam Hussein, Babylon is rising again."

[13] Revelation 18.

[14] http://almashriq.hiof.no/israel/300/320/327/israel-plo_recogni-

tion.html.

[15] Ellis Shuman, "Battle for the Temple Mount," israelinsider, July 30, 2001:   http://www.israelinsider.com/channels/security/articles/sec_0064.htm.

[16] http://www.wcg.org/wn/01april/national_association_of_evan-geli.htm.

PROPHETIC
TURNING POINTS

1. September 6, 605 BC · Nebuchadnezzar becomes king of the Babylonian Empire in present-day Iraq. This is the first of four great world empires identified in Daniel 2.
2. August 14, 586 BC · Nebuchadnezzar's troops burn Jerusalem. The nation of Israel no longer exists. God later gives the king a vision of four empires that are to rule the world until the end of time. The prophet Daniel interprets this dream for the king (Daniel 2).
3. October 12, 539 BC · Troops of Cyrus, king of Persia (modern-day Iran) enter Babylon. The first of the four world empires is gone. The second empire has taken over.
4. 539/538 BC · The prophet Daniel receives (Daniel 9) a revelation pinpointing the sequence of future events:

   • a decree will be issued to rebuild Jerusalem.
   • Jerusalem will be rebuilt.

- the Messiah will come at a specified time after the decree to rebuild Jerusalem.
- the Messiah will be "cut off."
- Jerusalem and its temple will be destroyed.
- a great ruler will arise from the people who destroyed the temple.
- the Jerusalem temple will stand again.
- the coming ruler will confirm a far-reaching agreement between nations.
- the coming ruler will betray his trust and dishonor the rebuilt temple.

5. March 5, 444 BC · Persian king Artaxerxes Longimanus issues a decree to rebuild Jerusalem, as prophesied by the prophet Daniel almost a century before. The nation of Israel is gradually re-established.

6. October 1, 331 BC · The Greek conqueror Alexander the Great defeats the Persians and gains their empire. The third World Empire takes over.

7. September 2, 31 BC · Roman troops defeat the Greeks, marking the end of the third empire prophesied in Daniel 2. The fourth empire, the Roman Empire, will never be replaced. When the Lord returns, the Roman Empire will again rule the earth.

8. March 30, AD 33 · Jesus Christ enters Jerusalem in His Triumphal Entry, revealing Himself to Israel as its Messiah on the date prophesied by Daniel over 600 years previously (Daniel 9:25).

9. April 3, AD 33 · Jesus is "cut off" as prophesied by Daniel 9:26. He is crucified, dies, and is buried. After three days, He comes back to life, but His people still reject Him.

10. August 5, AD 70 · Roman legions burn the Jerusalem temple, as prophesied in Daniel 9:26. The nation of Israel is destroyed. Most Jews are scattered throughout the world.

11. AD 476 · The barbarian leader Odoacer deposes the emperor at Rome. The Roman Senate formally hands over the empire to the ruler of eastern portion of the empire, whose headquarters are at Constantinople in present-day Turkey.

12. August 25, 570 · The traditional birth date of the prophet Muhammad. For almost 1400 years, Muhammad's religion, Islam, has tried to convert the world. It may play an important role in the events leading up to Jesus' return.

13. May 29, 1453 · The Muslim ruler Muhammad II conquers Constantinople, the capital of the Roman Empire since AD 476. The Roman Empire disappears. According to Daniel 9, this empire must reappear before Jesus returns.

14. May 8, 1945 · The Third Reich surrenders and World War II ends in Europe. Adolf Hitler's Third Reich, the last of three great attempts to resurrect the Roman Empire under German leadership, has collapsed. Hitler's plan to annihilate all Jews has failed.

15. August 6, 1945 · The age of weapons of mass destruction (WMD's) begins. An atomic bomb

is dropped on Hiroshima, Japan. For the first time, humans can inflict destruction like that described in the book of Revelation.

16. May 14, 1948 · The nation of Israel declares its independence. The prophecies of Ezekiel 38-39 and Daniel 9 begin to be fulfilled. Before Jesus comes back, the Jews will return to their land.

17. March 25, 1957 · The Treaty of Rome is signed, establishing the Common Market, today called the European Union. The Roman Empire of the last days, prophesied by Daniel, is coming into view.

18. June 7, 1967 · On the third day of the Six Day War, Israeli troops liberate Jerusalem's Temple Mount. For the first time in nearly 2,000 years, Jews control the site where Scripture says the temple will stand again.

19. September 11, 2001 · America receives a wake-up call. Muslim extremists attack New York's World Trade Center, the Pentagon in Washington, DC, and crash Flight 93 in rural Pennsylvania, killing thousands. With a jolt, the world moves closer to Armageddon.

CONTACT INFORMATION FOR JOHN W. NIEDER

Web Address: Johnonline.org
Email Address: john@johnonline.org
Mailing Address: Box 610350
                            Dallas, TX 75261